This charming and engaging mem who finds themselves at a crossroa to proceed. Rhona Morrison's sto and adventures on the high se and full of hope. The reader is en ....g... .. .. .p.... .. new opportunities, embrace them and to take an occasional leap of faith on their journey towards fulfilment. What a powerful, entertaining book.
– **Lorraine Kelly CBE**, broadcaster and author

Dr Rhona Morrison's latest work is a remarkable testament to the power of taking control of your own narrative and embracing life with purpose. This compelling book is filled with practical, real-life examples that inspire readers to navigate life's challenges with resilience and clarity. It will empower you to live a fulfilling life by responding thoughtfully to the world around you.
– **Pete Cooper**, career and talent specialist and author of
    The Better Human Blueprint

Rhona Morrison's latest book takes readers into the sad but familiar territory of bereavement and retirement with bounce, drive and optimism. It is packed with unsentimental anecdotes about the difficulties of facing bereavement and retirement together. You'll come to understand the importance of positive thought, planning, reaching out to friends, forcing yourself to business breakfasts at 6.30 am and working hard to fill that empty diary. A rich and varied read that tackles the difficult later-life circumstances that so many people face, with humour and an infectious sense of purpose.
– **Lesley Riddoch**, journalist, broadcaster and author

A poignant and entertaining memoir that beautifully explores resilience, hope and personal reinvention. Perfect holiday reading or for picking up when you need some inspiration!
– **Heather Suttie**, broadcaster and journalist, *Sunday Mail*

If you've reached some type of 'ending' in your life and are looking for some inspiration to help you navigate the next chapter, then this is for you. Rhona Morrison has written a beautiful, engaging and practically useful memoir of her journey from the simultaneous events of widowhood and retirement to becoming a globe-trotting author, artist and speaker. Her stories and observations about her adventures and mishaps had me chuckling and feeling exhilarated in equal measure.
– **Sarah Archer**, speaker, writer, performer and coach

A witty yet wise guide to navigating life's biggest transitions. With honesty, humility and plenty of humour, Dr Rhona Morrison shares the lessons she's learned from embracing change, facing loss and saying yes to unexpected opportunities. Whether you dream of travel, art, adventure, or simply a retirement filled with joy and purpose, this book will inspire you to design your own roadmap – without guilt, regret or waiting for permission.
– **Amy Rowlinson**, coach, podcaster and author of *Focus on Why*

A compelling and important piece of writing that brings our perception of mental health and wellbeing in everyday life front and centre – exactly where it needs to be. Elegantly combining challenging life circumstances with reflection, introspection and levity, this memoir will call you to take action in your own life. Simply wonderful.
– **Clarke Carlisle**, former Premier League footballer, PFA chair and MIND ambassador

FROM CRIME SCENES TO CRUISE SHIPS

Navigating life's troubled waters with resilience and hope

DR RHONA MORRISON

From Crime Scenes to Cruise Ships

ISBN 978-1-915483-81-2

eISBN 978-1-915483-82-9

Audio ISBN 978-1-915483-83-6

Published in 2025 by Right Book Press

Printed in the UK in June 2025

Manufactured by
Sue Richardson Associates Ltd.
Studio 6,
9, Marsh Street
Bristol
BS1 4AA

info@therightbookcompany.com

EU Safety Representative
eucomply OÜ
Parnu mnt 139b-14
11317 Tallinn
Estonia

hello@eucompliancepartner.com
+33 756 90241

Contents

Prologue

We all have dates that prove to be bookmarks in our lives, and mine was 23 March 2018. This was my 55th birthday; my retirement date from the National Health Service (NHS), where I'd worked as a consultant forensic psychiatrist for 32 years; and the day my husband Richard died from multiple inoperable brain tumours. I'd be entering a new chapter of life as a solo traveller, navigating bereavement while trying to forge a meaningful retirement. It wouldn't be the retirement I'd planned with my husband, but this next chapter didn't have to be a bad one – it would just be different. It has proved to be quite a journey so far.

In the past, I worked with mentally disordered murderers and rapists, and even have my very own stalker, who came to light when he interrupted a lecture I was delivering at my children's school, using a walkie-talkie that he'd planted underneath a grand piano. As you'll discover, even now, people still seem to want to follow me, but in a much less creepy way.

More than 30 years ago, I had to address the issue of a mentally disordered offender bringing a machete to his outpatient appointment. When I retired, I found myself sharing that story with more than 400 people on a cruise ship. It seems that, even in retirement, I was destined to talk about my passion.

Navigating change and major transitions in life can be challenging. There's inevitably a period of reassessment and readjustment as we strive to find our new place and purpose in the world. In my first book, *I Don't Talk to Dead Bodies: The curious encounters of a forensic psychiatrist* (published in 2022), my main objective, through sharing my anecdotes, was to encourage the reader to challenge their mindset around mental illness and offending, and contribute to the destig-matisation of mental illness. My main objective with this, my second book, is to highlight the importance of mindset in how we navigate major life transitions, whether they're planned (for example, marriage, parenthood, a new job or retirement), or unplanned (bereavement, life-limiting illness, divorce or redundancy). Inevitably, you'll have a new reality to adjust to.

At the end of each part of this book, I've taken time to reflect on what I've learned as I've navigated the changes in my personal life, in the hope that you may find some of my observations helpful when you next have to navigate a change in your own circumstances. I hope that by sharing my journey with you, you'll feel inspired and empowered to approach these inevitable changes in your life with an openness to embracing new possibilities and adventures. There may even be some curious encounters along the way...

PART 1

Life after loss

CHAPTER 1

Testing, testing, one, two, three...

'Good morning, thank you for joining me. Come on down to the front. I'll be starting in five minutes. Can you hear me OK up at the back?'

I can't believe I'm actually doing this. How did I get to be standing here on a five-star luxury cruise ship in Japan, lecturing about a book that I wrote? I'm a doctor, for God's sake! No one trained me to be an enrichment lecturer. I've never given a proper lecture on a stage, wearing a head mic, supported by a sound and lights technician in a booth up at the back.

Complete strangers have been invited to come and listen to what I have to say. What if I'm rubbish? What if I speak too fast, say 'um' and 'erm' too many times? What if I forget what I'm going to say next? What if they don't find the anecdotes amusing? What if I stop for a Q&A at the end and no one asks anything? What if they get up and leave halfway through? What if?... What if?... Stop!

Thank God, people are actually arriving for the lecture. The clock at the back says 10:58. It's nearly time. This is it. 'Welcome, my name is Dr Rhona Morrison. I'm a retired consultant forensic psychiatrist from Scotland and author of I Don't Talk to Dead Bodies: The curious encounters of a forensic psychiatrist.'

I hope this is the right button for the next slide... Phew... There it is. 'Today's lecture is called "Frogs and snails and puppy dog tails... What are forensic psychiatrists made of?".' When I introduce myself, people often hear the word forensic and automatically think CSI: Crime Scene Investigation, but I'm a forensic psychiatrist. It's a bit late if I turn up at the scene of a crime to try to interview a dead body! Let me explain what a forensic psychiatrist actually is and how I ended up choosing it as a career. It's not the obvious choice of profession when you're sitting having a chat with a careers advisor at school. Just to reassure you, the conversation with the careers advisor did not include "Are there any jobs where I can work with mentally ill murderers and rapists?" Frankly, that would have been weird!'

And I'm off. So far, the mic is working, I haven't collapsed, I've managed to work the IT system and no one has got up and left. Try not to speak too fast, Rhona; you know what you're like when you get into full flow during a story. When I tell my story about the emergency patient I saw one night – the bearded man who arrived wearing a tie over his bare chest and underpants over his trousers, talking to an imaginary fish finger – and I say to the audience, 'I wasn't expecting Superman', they laugh. My idea of trying to hook the audience in with witty anecdotes before delivering the underlying message about being non-judgemental about mental illness seems to be working. Thank God, my storytelling and key messages seem to be landing with the audience.

It's nearly 11:45, my material has filled the slot and I haven't run over. Phew. Oh, there are some hands up; people want to ask questions. Please ask me something I can answer! I hope there aren't any forensic psychologists in the audience. I always find them a bit intimidating because they always seem to quote research, statistics and specific high-profile cases, which isn't my style at all. I've found that there's often a bit of professional rivalry between psychiatrists and psychologists. Psychiatrists are medical doctors and psychologists are PhD doctors. Psychiatrists have usually had a very broad training, including delivering babies, assisting in operations, dealing with diabetes and cardiac arrests, as well as completing specialist psychiatry training, while psychologists have had a much more focused theoretical training in one specialty area. Psychiatrists diagnose and treat mental illness but also have to make sure they don't miss a brain tumour. Psychologists often deliver an evidence-based, focused intervention but, as well as diagnosing and treating the major mental illnesses, the psychiatrists retain overarching, long-term responsibility for the patient's medical care and are heavily involved with the multidisciplinary, holistic care package. We all bring specific skills, but mutual respect can sometimes be marred by judgemental attitudes. Have you heard of imposter syndrome? I think I've got it. It's self-doubt about your intellect, skills or accomplishments among high-achieving individuals. You feel as if you're not as talented or worthy as others and you're scared that one day you'll be found out by others to be incompetent.

There's a battle going on in my head between these irrational and rational thoughts. I always struggled with the idea of being called to court as an 'expert' witness, undervaluing my skills, expertise, training and clinical experience, despite working for more than 30 years as a specialist in the NHS, with multiple qualifications and courses to my name. Trying to tease that apart, I've always thought that an 'expert' is someone who's academic and can authoritatively quote facts, figures and research about a particular topic. I view myself as not particularly academic because I definitely can't quote facts, figures and research on my specialist topic. I do have the academic qualifications and training; I just can't quote the information chapter and verse. However, when I stand back, I'm able to challenge my own assumptions, as experts quoting academic data aren't always the best clinicians at the coal face, in terms of the soft people skills required to gain trust, take a detailed history or engage with the patient, to make a diagnosis, form a holistic care plan or a safe risk management plan. I was good at the latter, and that's essential in a good forensic psychiatry clinician.

I have many years of experience and expertise as a clinician working with mentally disordered offenders in a multitude of environments. I guess that makes me an expert, but the definition of expert in my head probably needs to be different, to allow me to truly own it. My expertise was more helpful in talking a paranoid man out of attacking a named victim in his delusional system with a machete, and persuading him to come quietly to hospital for some medication, rather than quoting the percentage chance of him actually murdering someone in his delusional system. Both have their place. I just need to value the expertise I do bring to the table. Can you see parallels in your own particular situation? Have you ever been promoted into a role that you're not actually trained for, such as taking on a managerial responsibility with a budget and HR responsibilities, when your training background and expertise to date is as a plumber or librarian? You may have felt a bit of an imposter with self-doubt, too.

Back at the lecture, I manage to quieten my mind and, fortunately, the audience questions aren't too detailed.

'Did you ever feel frightened?' That was easy to answer.

'How did you sleep at night?' That was easy to answer too.

'Do you think ADHD is more common now? Could it be linked to food additives?'

ADHD wasn't my area of expertise and I was confident enough to admit that. I learned this throughout my career. Safe doctors are the ones who know what they know and aren't afraid to ask a colleague when they don't know. Overconfident colleagues aren't always the best or safest doctors – they just have big egos!

'How do you manage your own stress?' Phew, I can answer that one.

And breathe. Microphone off. Unplug the laptop. I've survived delivering my first cruise line enrichment lecture. I think I can do this.

You may well be thinking, 'How on earth did you end up lecturing on a cruise ship?' Well, the journey from machetes to microphones has been an interesting ride. To tell that story, I need to wind back to 2018...

CHAPTER 2

So long, farewell...

As I wrote in the prologue, my husband Richard died on my 55th birthday, which was also my retirement day. It was a release for him, as he'd been losing a little bit more of himself and his function day by day; the tumours had been pressing against vital areas of his brain in the three months since his diagnosis. He was now at peace and for that I was grateful, but there was still the stark reality to deal with. You're on your own now, Rhona. Spreading out in front of me was a great big, empty void to fill.

The funeral arrangements were handled with the support of my daughter Jill, my son Fraser and Richard's sister Louisa. It's all a bit of a blur now, but in the space of a week we had to speak to the undertaker, choose flowers and a coffin, arrange funeral cars, speak to the minister at the church, register Richard's death, book the crematorium, arrange a eulogy, decide on the music, hymns and readings, arrange a reception in a local hotel for the wake, make a slideshow of photos, make copies of Fraser's CD for close family (he'd recorded himself singing three songs, to be played at the funeral, at his dad's request), buy plants for the tables and make little memorial plaques for them, make candle jars to decorate the church altar and hotel, and find appropriate outfits for me and the kids.

We were all operating on automatic pilot. There wasn't time to process the grief. We just had to attend to the practicalities of the situation. The funeral was to be held on 30 March 2018, Mum's 87th birthday. I don't think she expected her daughter to become a widow in her lifetime. My dad died just after he retired, too, so history was repeating itself. It's weird how these events impact you. You don't know until it happens. I was happy to accommodate the wishes of family members where I could, but oddly, I had a fixed view about the order of service. There's usually a photograph of the deceased on the front, and so it would be for Richard, but I had an overwhelming desire to put a photo of both of us on the front. We'd been together through thick and thin for 38 years and I wanted to be with him, right by his side, until the end. It was such an overwhelmingly strong feeling, clearly not open to negotiation, so we were pictured together.

After we'd all contributed memories and ideas, Louisa wrote the eulogy. She wrote it well and the minister delivered a very personal tribute to Richard as a result. I'll never forget Fraser's rich, baritone voice echoing around the church and at the crematorium, as they played the songs he'd pre-recorded, each with such personal meaning: 'Caledonia' (a nod to Richard's Scottish heritage), 'Moon River' (our wedding waltz), and 'For Good' (from the musical Wicked, which reminded us that we'd been changed for good as a result of knowing him, which was so poignant to hear).

It was overwhelming to see hundreds of friends and family arriving to say their final farewell and offer condolences. All the dilemmas we'd had during the days before the funeral drifted into oblivion. We got through it. In the end, I walked down the aisle on my own, so that other family members each had someone by their side. Walking back up the aisle with hundreds of faces all staring in my direction was a bit surreal, but it was a case of one foot in front of the other, and I got there.

Richard's cousins from Shetland and the US had made the trip, which meant a lot, and there were also his work colleagues, badminton players, tennis players, neighbours, my old colleagues, friends and family, all hugging and shaking our hands outside the church. The outpouring of love was overwhelming. My university pal, William, having travelled all the way up from Blackpool, in north-west England, appeared in the line-up as a surprise. He didn't need to do it, but that hug from an old friend meant the world. We've kept in touch since. People cared and were looking out for me and the kids. The future was going to be OK.

A funeral is the final goodbye, which gives some closure, but our goodbyes had been protracted during Richard's illness. We'd said goodbye to each other every time there was a stepwise loss of function, mourning a future that would never be. The funeral became a celebration of his life. It was a time to share memories and reminisce, to give us something to hold on to. My neighbours told funny anecdotes that made me laugh. One was about an overnight trip we took to Loch Lomond. Everyone remembered Richard complaining to the management of the country club because there were no fried potato scones on the breakfast buffet. If you ever visit Scotland and have a cooked breakfast, make sure you sample the fried potato scones (my favourite), black pudding and haggis, but don't ask for the recipe before you eat the last two! Richard was known for his skills as an accomplished complainer. Occasionally, even now, I find myself attempting to channel Richard, as I'm not the best at making complaints.

I had another moment when I found myself being very clear in my opinions, and that was just after the cremation. The beautiful flower arrangement on top of the coffin was removed before the cremation took place and was going to be left on the ground outside the chapel of rest and eventually get eaten by deer or rabbits. I wanted to take the flowers to the hotel, then take them home, which I did. It was like holding on just a little bit longer. When I eventually put the wilting flowers in the garden waste recycling bin a couple of weeks later, it felt wrong, as if I was throwing away a bit of Richard. I hadn't quite thought that through, but it felt so important and non-negotiable on the day of the funeral.

It's funny what our brains do when we're stressed. I'd always thought that grief comes after the funeral, once the practical tasks have been done. People often dissociate their emotions for a while to cope with the essential arrangements. However, it wasn't really like that for me and it surprised me quite a bit. Even now, almost seven years later, as I've been writing, I've experienced brief surges of emotion, like fizz rising to the top of a bottle and escaping. I go into a temporary state of sadness with a lump in my throat and tears in my eyes, but then it settles. It happened the other day when my gas fire, internet and printer all decided to stop working at the same time. I'm a bit of a technophobe, so I quickly felt overwhelmed and acutely aware of Richard's absence. He would've had it fixed in minutes. There were tears. Certain memories still trigger these emotions, but I've never had a period of consistently low mood or overwhelming sadness. I genuinely believe my grief was more of a slow burn of coming to terms with the reality of what we were facing together during Richard's final months. I had plenty of time to process and prepare myself for what was coming down the line and it definitely softened the blow. Obviously, we both felt cheated, but we had no regrets and lots to be thankful for. That allowed me to feel at peace, and for that I'm grateful.

I've never learned how to play the strategic game of chess. I don't think I'd have the concentration for it as I'm too easily distracted. But I do know the way the knight chess piece moves, due to 'knight's move thinking' being a symptom of schizophrenia. This is when someone's thinking unexpectedly goes off at a tangent and is difficult to follow. I thought I had a bit of a strategy and plan for retirement, and then I didn't. A greater force had decided not only to move the pieces on the chessboard of my life, but to remove my king, Richard, altogether. My long-term game plan and strategy no longer fitted. I was going to be playing a different game: solitaire.

The NHS offers clinicians pre-retirement seminars to assist with retirement planning, but I'd missed out as I'd had to leave work to become a full-time carer for Richard. True to form, I didn't read any articles about the topic and just stumbled blindly into the abyss, hoping I could use my positive mindset as a parachute.

CHAPTER 3

The empty chair

One of my biggest regrets is that Richard wasn't around to witness the growth and blossoming of Jill and Fraser into the successful, capable adults they are today. When your children are born, it's difficult to prevent your mind from wandering to the future, imagining all the opportunities and major milestones they may have ahead of them. Now that Richard's life has been cut short, it's the children who are left imagining what it might have been like to share their successes with their dad. There's definitely an empty chair at our family table. But he would've been so proud of them.

Jill moved from her first flat into a lovely mid-terrace home, acutely aware that in the past her dad had always been there at important times in her life, able to offer practical support and knowledge. Who'd be hanging the curtains and putting up shelves now? She picked up the keys on her own this time. She's gone on to decorate and furnish her home with flair. Not a wall, floor, kitchen or bathroom remained the same once she got her hands on it. Her philosophy is that if you buy good quality, it lasts, but that means she's always putting something on her credit card! Richard was always a supporter of Jill's sporting achievements in swimming, skiing and hockey. How proud he'd have been to see her cycle across Cuba, fundraising in his memory.

Fraser bought his first three-bedroom mid-terrace home after his dad died and surprised all of us with his amazing attention to detail. His house looked like a show home two days after moving in. He worked his way up in Young Enterprise Scotland to manage the flagship Senior Schools Programme, which teaches entrepreneurial skills across the whole of Scotland. He developed the programme further until the content was accredited as a qualification. Then he digitised everything, which allowed the programme to continue online during the pandemic. He grew his team and was heavily involved with marketing and managing volunteers. During this time, he completed a leadership skills programme and completed his BA in business and enterprise at Edinburgh Napier University. Another proud mum moment came on graduation day. Richard had been worried when Fraser left university after only six weeks to start his own business. But it seems that timing is everything. Fraser was much more motivated to study when he felt it had a purpose and would aid his career progression. I thought he'd stay in this line of work, as he seemed to be thriving. However, one day he told me he was thinking of applying for a new job. Weeks before, he'd directed the musical *Sunshine on Leith* at the new theatre in Cumbernauld, with the Cumbernauld Musical Theatre Society, which he founded and directed. It was a sellout, standing-ovation triumph over six shows.

The theatre has been Fraser's passion since the age of seven, but he believed he needed a qualification in the arts to pursue it. However, he finally opted for a different career path, choosing to pursue performing and directing at a high-quality, amateur level. Then the job of creative producer was advertised at the Cumbernauld Theatre. He told me he'd apply, as the CEO had seen the quality of his directing, which by anyone's standards is professional, despite technically being amateur. He had more experience of planning, performing, producing, directing, preparing lighting plots, musical directing, set design, budgeting and conducting auditions for theatre productions than anyone coming out of university with a degree in the arts. The interview went really well and he got his dream job, working in a brand-new theatre. He was in his element. He'd also get free tickets to even more shows, as theatre companies like creative producers to see their shows and hopefully add them to their programme.

In the summer of 2023, he went to see 32 shows at the Edinburgh Fringe Festival. What made it particularly special was that he sent me a long text, which was highly unusual, as he's normally a man of few text words. He invited me to attend three shows in one day, which would also be an opportunity to meet his new girlfriend. Double take... Wind back... New girlfriend?! He'd never mentioned a girlfriend! I was definitely going now. Alisa is lovely: friendly, calm and relaxed. She fits right in and they have more in common than I'd anticipated. She works as a doctor in Edinburgh. When I asked how they met, I couldn't believe my ears. During her medical training she visited a forensic psychiatry service in Australia. What were the chances of that? On return she noticed my memoir being promoted on Facebook and bought it. She recognised Fraser's photo inside the cover because 14 years earlier they'd both asked their respective parents if they could audition for the child cast of the professional pantomime at the Macrobert Arts Centre in Stirling, and had been successful. They'd done this for two consecutive years. They were at different schools but made friends and Alisa helped to teach Fraser the dance steps as she was a dancer. Here they were, 14 years later, and their paths were about to cross again. She contacted him via Facebook and they arranged to meet. Clearly they hit it off and the rest, as they say, is history. They subsequently moved in together and Fraser inherited Alisa's two cats, Jess and Wallace.

He's become a cat dad and is besotted! It's so lovely to see him in a happy, stable relationship and I'll watch with interest to see what their future holds. I feel really proud that my book played its part in bringing them together. Fraser has now moved jobs to take on the challenge of becoming executive and creative director at Eastgate Theatre in Peebles, which makes me extremely proud.

As I continue my journey, no longer part of a duo, I'm constantly discovering everything that Richard took care of behind the scenes, often unknown to me and therefore unrecognised, and with hindsight, not appreciated as it should have been. Whether it was organising insurance, paying road tax, arranging lawn treatments, renewing the TV licence, replacing flickering light bulbs, making travel plans, washing the car, filling up the screen wash, fixing the computer or getting the car serviced, it just miraculously happened. I had no idea what needed to be done, when it had to be done, how much it would cost or whether we had a direct debit in place to deal with it, and I lacked the practical skills for anything technical. When I reflect on why this was, my only defence is that I was working hard to earn the money we needed to sustain our lifestyle and abdicating responsibility for the practical and financial household tasks to Richard, except for the cooking, ironing and cleaning. He was quite traditional! He never found his way around the kitchen, except for boiling the kettle to make a cup of coffee.

My top tip would be that, however you split the tasks within a relationship, always maintain a healthy awareness of everything that needs to happen around the home and know where to find the passwords, just in case you find yourself having to take over responsibility for the tasks at some point. Clearly, I didn't practise what I preach.

CHAPTER 4

Navigating bereavement

I f you google articles about the stages of grief, some say that there are five, some seven, but essentially they follow the same pattern. However, I believe that the timing of the process will affect the journey. If someone close to you has a life-limiting illness or a slowly declining memory, you have some warning and can prepare for bereavement. You may even start the grieving process before the person dies as you may be losing a little piece of them a day at a time. It was like that for me with Richard. On our journey from that shock diagnosis to his death three months later, we lost a little bit more of him every day.

They say that the seven stages of grief are: shock, denial, anger, bargaining, depression, acceptance and hope, and finally, processing the grief. Sadly, for a minority, there's a more prolonged grief reaction that may last more than a year after the loss, but the majority will make progress before then. However, despite there being no average timetable for grief, the stages described will be familiar to many people who have experienced the grieving process. We're unlikely to avoid it; it's the circle of life.

The American–Swiss psychiatrist Elisabeth Kübler-Ross first described five stages of grief in her 1969 book *On Death and Dying*. Initially, her model was based on people coming to terms with terminal illness but it was later adapted as a way to think about grief in general. Some suggestions were subsequently made to include a further two stages. The stages need not be linear and there may be triggers along the way that may temporarily set you back, reminding you all too acutely of your loss and the emotions that come with it. I used to see a man walking down the street and mistake him for my dead father because of the pattern of hair loss and similar clothing, or find myself automatically drawn to the children's clothes section in Littlewoods department store, where I used to find stretchy clothes that would fit my disabled sister, Vivienne, and then remember 'I'll not be needing these anymore' after she died at the age of 23. Understanding the stages that may be encountered during grief can help to make sense of the fluctuating emotional journey, which will be unique to everyone. You may never encounter some of the stages at all and some may overlap. Here's how it worked for me.

1. Shock

Richard's shock diagnosis on the day that he had a CT scan in December 2017 was the start of my grief journey. I'd feared that there was something neurological underlying his recent dizziness, unsteadiness and mild memory impairment, but I wasn't expecting the conversation with a junior doctor, just after the scan, when we were told 'You've got three tumours in your brain, Richard', followed by his immediate hospitalisation. In that moment I knew deep down in the pit of my stomach that we were going to lose him and I'd have to support him through a difficult journey. I felt a bit numb. There's often a sense of numbness, with no outward show of emotion at this stage. This detachment from feelings is something I'd experienced a lot before as a psychiatrist. I'd had to keep going, despite sometimes unimaginable information being shared with me regarding traumatic experiences or detailed information about heinous crimes. I still remember being asked to watch a CCTV recording, sent to me by a lawyer, which had captured the attempted murder of his intoxicated client. The perpetrator punched the victim, who fell to the ground unconscious. He then stood back and took aim, kicking the victim's head as if he were taking a penalty. The victim's body was limp, like a rag doll, but his head rolled from side to side before gradually coming to a stop. It was horrific. That stands out as one of the worst things I can remember. I sat in complete silence, horrified by what had just played out in front of me, unable to speak, and then I just felt numb. Emotional detachment allowed me to maintain my composure and do my job in many situations, despite probably being in shock. Perhaps that was what kicked in after the scan as I tried to support Richard and decide how to break the news to the kids and Richard's sister before they visited him later that evening.

2. Denial

Sometimes people accept that something has happened, but it doesn't feel real or they struggle to believe it. Feeling numb is common then, too. In Richard's case, he was starting to grieve for a future that was going to be denied him, but rather than being in denial, there was a calm acceptance. I don't think I experienced this denial stage. My medical head was the one in charge, recognising and accepting the sad trajectory ahead and starting to process what it meant for everyone around me, including myself.

3. Anger

Anger affects everyone differently. Some feel angry at being left behind by a loved one who's died, some feel angry with themselves for struggling to process what has happened, some feel angry that death has stolen the future they'd planned, feeling as if their loved one has died before their time, and so on. It isn't always an easy emotion to process with other family members, as they're all on their own journey, trying to process the grief. We may fear upsetting them by talking about it. Finding someone to talk to outside the family can allow a more open and honest space for processing the emotion, without fear of judgement or negative consequences for others who are also grieving. There was quite a lot of discussion with Richard as he felt angry that he was being denied his future with me and the kids and that illness was denying him his retirement. Both of our fathers were denied their retirement too, dying all too soon and never getting to know their grandchildren. I felt angry that our joint plans for retirement wouldn't come to fruition. However, both of us were consoled by the fact that we'd had 38 happy years together, produced two lovely children and travelled the world extensively as a family. We hadn't put off travel 'until retirement'. We'd lived our lives and made memories, which would now be cherished. Some people feel angry that they weren't afforded time to say what needed to be said and to put things in place. We were fortunate to have some time, albeit limited. I'm not going to deny that having a best friend who's a psychotherapist has its advantages in terms of processing grief. Thank you, Alison.

4. Bargaining

This may be the 'what if?' stage, where we ask ourselves if the outcome could've been altered, if only we'd done something different. For example, the wife of a smoker who died of lung cancer may ask, 'What if I'd insisted he stopped smoking when I was pregnant 30 years ago?' Or, 'Would it have made a difference if I'd encouraged him to go to the doctor six months ago when he coughed up some blood?' It may also be a chance to make promises or look for a chance to make things right. They might commit to stopping smoking themselves as they want to see their grandchildren grow up. People may search for reasons when there are none and feel perhaps they are to blame. Richard quickly said, 'It's not fair,' but he didn't have any regrets about the way he'd lived his life.

5. Depression

As a psychiatrist, I'm all too familiar with the symptoms people may experience when they're depressed, eg low mood, insomnia, loss of appetite, poor concentration, lack of motivation, feelings of hopelessness, lethargy, feelings of guilt or low self-worth, so I was on the lookout for these in myself, but they didn't come. I think the fact that we had three months to process Richard's diagnosis meant that I was afforded time to gradually adjust to the fact that I was going to lose him. As his faculties began to be affected and he experienced impaired mobility, balance, speech, manual dexterity, vision and incontinence, we encountered loss on a daily basis, knowing that we were progressing, one faltering step at a time, towards the end. As we approached the day he died, we were both resigned and didn't want the suffering to be protracted. It was a relief for us both when he slipped away with dignity, sleeping in his own bed, no longer suffering. I didn't feel depressed after he died. I was happy that he hadn't suffered for too long and we'd been afforded enough time as a family to say what we needed to say and to plan for the future. We had no regrets and lots of good memories. We were the lucky ones. For those who experience debilitating depression after a bereavement, they may feel that life has no meaning and even have thoughts that they want to join their loved one. It's important in this instance to seek professional help to get through the process (see the 'Useful resources' section at the end of the book for some suggestions.)

6. Acceptance and hope

This stage will be different for everyone, but social contact with friends and family helps us to move forward. It doesn't mean we've forgotten the deceased person, but the realisation that we can't change what has happened coexists with the need to navigate a future that isn't yet written, and we can take strength from the fact that we have some control over that. Some feel guilty for laughing and having fun when a loved one has died. I always felt that Richard would've wanted us to be happy and live our lives. The distraction of social activity and friendships helps, but it doesn't mean we don't experience reflective moments when our grief is still immensely over-whelming, often in bed at night on our own, when we're still trying to process our loss and there's an empty pillow beside us. That was how it was for me, anyway. I've always described myself as someone who tries to see the positives, learning from any situation, even if it feels quite negative. This mindset inevitably coloured my bereavement journey. When I write a card after someone loses a loved one, I almost always say, 'They may have gone from your midst, but they will remain in your heart forever.'

7. Processing grief

The process of grieving is highly individual, so it's important not to compare yourself with other people and give yourself the time you need. One article I read recently suggested a series of strategies to cope with grief, for example: expressing your grief in words or art; connecting with others (including support groups, if necessary); not being afraid to ask for help; deep breathing; setting small, achievable goals; looking after your health (sleep, exercise, diet); and practising how to respond to questions about your situation. I didn't read any articles at the time but I did do some of the things on the list. I wrote about my journey as part of writing my memoir, and within that I covered my adjustment to Richard's illness and eventual death. That was cathartic. There were lots of tears. I used art as an outlet, both expressively and as a social outlet, which also gave structure to my day. I used family and friends to help provide a social structure and support. I even did some training in functional breathing, which can improve stress management, performance and sleep. I set goals in terms of my art and writing, joined various groups, started playing tennis and tried to develop my social circle following retirement. I also made plans to travel, so there were lots of distractions. All these actions helped to steer me on a positive path towards accepting what had happened and finding a fulfilling future plan as a solo traveller in life. There isn't a right or a wrong way, just your own personal way of making sense of the world and creating a social structure that supports and energises you.

CHAPTER 5

In memory – ashes to ashes

Everyone reacts differently in response to grief, how they remember a loved one and how they show gratitude to those who've helped them in their time of need. Although we managed Richard's final weeks and days as a family, as Richard wanted to be at home during his final days, latterly we were supported by the Strathcarron Hospice at Home team. Jill, Fraser and I all wanted to show our gratitude, in memory of Richard, by supporting the fundraising efforts for the hospice, and we all used our own particular skills to do that.

Jill has always been a sporty thrill-seeker, so it was no surprise that she chose to be sponsored to abseil down the Forth Rail Bridge and the Falkirk Wheel (both local landmarks), zip wire across the River Clyde and then cycle across Cuba with her friend Kirsty. They'd originally planned to climb Mount Kilimanjaro but Kirsty's subsequent knee surgery meant this activity was off the cards. What adventures she had raising money for this worthy cause.

Fraser, our talented entertainer, arranged a fundraising concert with his friends in the Old Kirk in Kirkcaldy. He and his musical theatre buddies have run biannual concerts there for several years and have raised more than £26,000 for several local charities close to the hearts of the group members. They opted to fundraise for the hospice after Richard died. Fraser continued to rise to the challenge of fundraising at a time when in-person concerts were no longer possible. His efforts were outstanding. He put together a full two-hour programme of solos and four-part harmony group numbers. His friend Alan recorded the music, then Fraser recorded videos of himself conducting. The videos were sent to the choir members so they could learn their parts, then video themselves singing their part and return it to Fraser. He then had the mammoth task of collating all the videos and individual soundtracks to produce a cohesive virtual concert. It was advertised on social media with a link to a fundraising page where people could donate to the group's chosen charity for each concert. In addition, they recorded songs to cheer people up on a weekly basis during lockdown.

I've since met several of the choir members at musical theatre shows and their feedback about being part of the choir was overwhelmingly about how much it benefited their mental health to be part of this shared musical theatre activity. Contact and communication are the first steps to letting someone know that you value and care about them. Even now, I cherish handwritten letters and greetings cards popping through my letterbox. It's difficult to quantify just how impactful a simple text or phone call from friends can be when you find yourself adjusting to the new reality of being on your own. I was fortunate to have lots of support.

As for me, I used my artistic talents to fundraise. The hospice has an annual Snowdrop Appeal, so I designed a snowdrop greetings card, drawn with pen-and-ink pointillism with splodges of turquoise ink, using the hospice's colours, and I also used turquoise envelopes. All proceeds went to the hospice. I also agreed to hang framed prints of my artwork in the hospice itself, and a percentage of these sales goes to the hospice on an ongoing basis. With approximately £15,000 worth of fundraising required every day to keep the hospice running, all efforts are greatly appreciated.

Writing my memoir was part of my celebration of Richard's life as he was an integral part of my journey from age 17 through to 55. It captures a taste of our many happy memories together. He'd be amazed by some of the adventures I've had since he died. In reality, most of my adventures wouldn't have happened if he were still here. Our travel would've been curtailed by his cardiomyopathy, which seriously constrained his ability to walk any distance without becoming fatigued. We would've spent a happy retirement together, with probably a few too many cakes in garden centre coffee shops, but that door has sadly firmly closed. With my usual glass-half-full mentality, I've risen to the challenge and taken the opportunities afforded to me at a time of adversity and just gone for it.

I decided to keep the family timeshare in Ballater so I could carry on taking annual holidays there and eventually pass it on to the kids. It's a spot that holds such fond memories from all our annual winter holidays over more than 30 years – sledging with Granny, horse riding at Glentanner, quad biking in Aboyne, the kids learning to ski, walks by the river and jigsaws at the lodge. It seemed the obvious place to scatter some of Richard's ashes, so we made a pilgrimage north as a family group and walked to the remote Loch Muick setting that so typifies the beauty and majesty of the Highlands of Scotland. The loch is surrounded by mountains and hikers' paths, with herds of wild deer roaming on the hillside, looking resplendent with their antlers. It's about an 11-mile drive from Ballater, involving a long stretch along a one-track road with passing places before you reach a car park in the middle of nowhere.

For those of you who are interested in the difference between a loch and a lake, it has to do with where they're located. In Scotland, we call them lochs (the Gaelic word for lake). Loch Muick is an upland freshwater loch that lies about five miles south of Braemar, within the boundary of the Balmoral estate (where Balmoral Castle, the summer residence of King Charles and Queen Camilla, is located). It takes approximately three hours to walk around the loch and it's a moderately challenging route in places. Be warned, if you're unfit like me, it takes longer. If you tire halfway round, too bad, because there's no easy way back. That was my discovery. You just have to keep going! It's so remote and unspoilt. Due to accessibility issues, it will never be developed commercially.

Jill scratched 'DAD' and a love heart on the sandy loch shore before we stood together on a little wooden footbridge over the river that flows out of the loch and said our goodbyes for the last time. He'll never be forgotten. Ballater was the last place Richard had wanted to visit, just a matter of weeks before his death. Jill and I took him, but it was challenging, as his balance had gone, he was in a wheelchair, and the living area, bedroom and shower room he'd be using were up a full flight of stairs. We made it happen to honour his wishes, but it was physically and emotionally exhausting. It was so distressing, knowing that he was saying his own private goodbye to our special place. It still upsets me to recall him sitting in the restaurant in the country club, in his wheelchair, quietly looking around the room, committing every detail to memory, knowing that he'd never come back. Even now, it makes me cry to think of that moment.

I travel back to Ballater every year, but rather than have an empty seat at the table, I've visited with friends so that I can share the beauty of Royal Deeside. My university friends, Alison and Jane, came up to celebrate Jane's 60th birthday. I had a few days at the start on my own, under bright turquoise skies, but when they arrived midweek it was snowing. Then we were snowed in and they couldn't return home. The kids were planning to join me for the weekend, but the snow gates were closed, so that plan was abandoned too. They say you can experience four seasons in one day in Scotland, and we certainly had a week of mixed fortunes.

In 2024, I took my friend Morag for her 60th-birthday

treat. She used to own a holiday lodge there and had actually introduced me and Richard to the area. We loved it so much that we bought our own lodge. It was lovely to reminisce and revisit memories and old haunts that we'd both shared with Richard three decades earlier. The next visitor will be fellow psychiatrist Anne, to celebrate her 65th birthday. Our friendship dates back to our psychiatry training days in the late 1980s.

When you walk into the lodge, it feels like a big, warm hug. I instantly relax, get out a book and a jigsaw and the pace of life slows right down. It always feels as if I've just returned home. It's not so easy to visit as a family anymore, but it will always have a special place in our hearts.

Reflections on life after loss

When you've been with the same partner for more than 30 years, it's easy to become complacent and imagine that your future together is all mapped out. I'd never really contemplated being on my own. What I needed was a game plan, as the goalposts had suddenly moved. No, that doesn't quite cover it. I felt as if I'd been transported onto a completely different playing field.

Becoming a widow on my 55th birthday is probably the biggest life transition I've ever had to navigate, especially as it happened on the same day as my retirement from the NHS. I believe that how we view a situation affects how we deal with it, both practically and emotionally. My glass-half-full view of the world meant that I chose to celebrate the positive times I had with Richard rather than dwell on the plans that had been stolen from us.

When I was working as a forensic psychiatrist, I was regularly required to reframe difficult situations for patients and families in an attempt to give hope or closure. The challenge I now faced was to find my own closure. My main conclusions were that I needed to be thankful for the 38 years I had with Richard and for the memories we made.

I had no regrets, but I do remember making a fundamental promise to myself after he died and that was to live my life and make every day count, as you don't know what's ahead of you. I've embraced this promise to myself wholeheartedly and hope that I'm being a good role model for my children and those around me.

I guess my advice would also be to embrace the liberation that comes from being a solo traveller in life, regardless of how you arrived there. You have fewer constraints and less need to compromise. Pursue what makes you feel happy and energised, and the issues you feel passionate about. The first step is to give yourself permission to be happy and fulfilled. We only get one shot at this life. I told myself, 'I'm still here, so I need to live life to the fullest.' This will inevitably look different for everyone.

The future may not be what you'd planned, but the next chapter of life doesn't have to be a difficult one. What I've concluded is that there's no right way or roadmap to follow for bereavement, retirement or any other change in life circumstances. Forging your own path, based on what makes you feel fulfilled, is what will work for you. Don't worry what other people think about you embracing life, as they're probably jealous!

In this next chapter of my life, I'm committed to being open to all opportunities as none of us knows what the future holds. I wonder whether you employ a similar mindset as a coping strategy? If not, it might be helpful to try to reframe a tricky situation that you may be facing by trying to focus on the positives, whether that be identifying learning points for use in the future or trying to identify things to celebrate or be thankful for.

PART 2

Filling the retirement void

CHAPTER 6

Friends united

My friends Alison and Derek took me out for dinner a week after Richard's funeral and told me they had something delicate to discuss. We'd had to cancel a joint pre-retirement luxury cruise from Singapore to Hong Kong a few months earlier because Richard was too ill to travel. We'd had to persuade Alison and Derek to go on the cruise without us. The cruise line was very understanding and subsequently sold me retrospective insurance, which protected the large sum of money that had been tied up in the cruise. However, it meant that at some point I'd need to go on a cruise myself. That was an uncomfortable conversation to have with Richard in the weeks before he died, as he'd not be going. Initially, when we'd cancelled the first one, he'd said that perhaps we could go on a river cruise instead, which wouldn't involve flying. He didn't realise just how unwell he was at that point. Taking out the retrospective insurance was the right thing to do. However, it did focus both of us on the reality of our situation and me on my future on my own.

Alison and Derek informed me they'd booked a holiday with the same luxury cruise line for early 2019, on a small ship. They told me I was going with them, no discussion, but I'd need to book it soon as the ship was already nearly full. It was such a generous offer for me to accompany them on my first solo trip, but I was worried about what people might think about me booking a holiday just weeks after Richard died. I decided to discuss it with the kids and, if I had their blessing, I'd book it, but wouldn't discuss it with anyone else until a bit of time had passed. The kids were 100 per cent on board with the idea, saying that I deserved it and Dad would want me to go. And so it was booked, including additional nights at either end. We'd be away for four and a half weeks in total. Alison and Derek said it was too long a flight to go straight to Australia to board our cruise ship, which was ultimately bound for New Zealand. They wanted me to have a taste of the Far East, from the cruise I'd missed with Richard.

With the funeral behind me, I found myself with a huge retirement void to fill. Our joint plans had been shattered into tiny pieces. I'd thought about going to watercolour art classes, just to have some social contact and get my eye in again after a 38-year gap since sitting my higher art exam at school. After doing a brief bit of research, I chose Art 4 You, as it was about a 40-minute drive away from my home. The pleasant country drive to and from the class meant more time filled in my empty diary. As a lifelong, busy multitasker, I didn't relish having any blank pages.

I decided to go to art class every week and sat next to a lady called Lisa. I met some lovely people and enjoyed my return to creativity. Eventually, some of us would become friends and meet up socially for lunch outside class. Our teacher, Frances, was a talented watercolourist but had a very different style to mine. She was using watercolours in the way they were intended to be used, but my own style rapidly emerged, with my preference being to create detailed images depicting light, dark, reflections, buildings, harbours, trees, landscapes or animals. I'd do a pencil drawing first, with detail, detail and more detail, and then use very small brushes to complete the painting. There wasn't a lot of water involved!

One week, I was unable to attend class due to a clashing commitment. As I'd paid for a block of sessions, the teacher told me to pop along to an alternative class. I turned up at an acrylics class with no idea about what I'd be doing. Shortly after the session began, I heard the door to the studio open behind me, the latecomer announcing, 'Sorry I'm late. My name is Anna. Where should I sit?' That soft Lancashire accent was all too familiar. It was my friend from university. We'd once shared 'Albert', the dead body we dissected in anatomy classes. I turned around and our eyes met in disbelief, shortly followed by the longest hug. 'How's Richard?' With a gap of more than 30 years since we'd left university, she had no idea that Richard had died, although she'd known him well. She called her husband in the middle of the class. 'Angus, I've just met lovely Rhona. Richard died. She's coming for dinner; get the barbecue on.'

That was a pivotal moment. Our friendship was rekindled, never to be extinguished again. Since that initial reconnection, we've gone on to have meals together, trips to art galleries and the Edinburgh Fringe Festival, gone for walks on the golf course, painted together, had trips to the theatre and, during my 60th birthday year, she and Angus generously invited me to join them for a glorious holiday at their holiday home in the south of France. True friendships were forged during the shared experience of medical school, so we found ourselves fitting right back into an easy relationship where the conversation flowed effortlessly. At university, Anna, a Lancashire farmer's daughter, had announced that she wanted to marry a 'Scotsman in a kilt', but no suitable candidate emerged until after graduation. When she phoned to invite me to her wedding, she told me Angus, her husband to be, went to school in Kirkintilloch. So did I! It turned out that Angus was in my primary five reading group at school, so I've actually known him longer than Anna. What are the chances of that?!

I eventually left the art class, having decided to build an art studio in my back garden. It felt self-indulgent to spend so much money on a hobby, but I decided that a studio made of UPVC, with double glazing and electricity, was a much better (although more costly) option for a single female, as maintenance of a wooden garden outbuilding was not my forte and frankly an unattractive prospect. It also meant it could be used all year round.

I became a prolific producer of artwork and soon found myself with a huge pile of paintings that I didn't know what to do with. This stage occurred only a few months after the studio had been built. I started to feel guilty, this time because I realised I was financially secure and could literally get up every day and do whatever I wanted. This didn't sit well with 'Rhona the doctor', who'd spent 38 years caring for people. I talked it through with my best friend Alison, the psychotherapist. She always knows what to ask and how to frame her responses to get me to a point of self-discovery and clarity. She said, 'Have you considered selling them? That way there would be a purpose to your art and you wouldn't feel so guilty.' We continued the discussion over the course of several months, during which Fraser said he'd set up a Facebook page and build me a website for my business. Until that point I'd avoided social media as I didn't want patients contacting me or knowing my business. I also had my own personal stalker to consider (for that whole story, you'll have to read my first book).

The kids suggested arranging an open-studio event at the house. That was a nerve-racking idea. Would anyone come or want to buy anything? Was my art any good? It wasn't about making money; it was about legitimising my activity and getting rid of the growing mountain of artwork. I advertised it to my friends and on my Rhona Morrison Art Facebook page. Around 50 people turned up and I sold about £900 worth of art in three hours, so maybe there was something in this art malarkey after all. And so the art business was born. It was never going to make me much money or make me famous, but it gave me some purpose and helped to fill the blank diary. My return to art had proved to be quite therapeutic and life enhancing for many different reasons.

CHAPTER 7

Look before you leap
– or don't!

As the old proverb says, 'Look before you leap.' I genuinely believe that's good advice, especially as one of my patients once leapt over a wall and broke their leg when they discovered there was a 10 ft drop on the other side. They were escaping an attack from a gang member with a machete at the time, so in their eyes it may have been worth it. I can't remember the circumstances now. However, despite it being good advice, I don't think I'm the best role model in this regard, as I can be quite impulsive. I'm not one for being reckless, as I'm actually quite risk averse, but I do tend to sign up for non-risky things without reading the small print and sometimes find myself embroiled in more than I bargained for.

I once signed up for a business coaching course at work, assuming it would be a two- or three-day course. It went on for nine months, involving several days of training, weekly coaching and a long-term commitment to join the NHS coach bank afterwards. Fortunately, I loved it, and it greatly enhanced my skill set. But if I'd read the blurb in advance, I wouldn't have signed up, due to the time commitment. I never read instruction manuals either. I tend to glaze over by page two! The skills that I learned were helpful for coaching staff, but they also enhanced my own problem-solving skills and my ability to challenge myself if I'm allowing assumptions to cloud my judgement and decision making.

I'd been toying with writing my memoir before retirement and had started to jot down random anecdotes while I was off work caring for Richard. He slept a lot, so it passed the time. When he died, I decided it was one of the things I could do to fill my time. What did I know about writing a memoir? A big fat zero! I hadn't done a creative writing course; I didn't know how to include meaningful dialogue, or what a consistent, authentic voice was. I didn't know if there were rules about structure or what to include. Following an online search for courses, I came across an advert for an annual, one-week residential memoir-writing course at Moniack Mhor, the creative writing centre in Inverness. It was due to take place in about six weeks' time and there was one place left. I also found an advert for a university lecturer who held residential writing retreats at her cottage in Inverness. She offered to read and critique a few thousand words of your manuscript and give written feedback.

There was no looking before leaping. The course only happened once a year, so I signed up for both and headed up to Inverness. I'd never driven that far by myself, so that was a first, too. Richard had always been the driver on long journeys. This would be one of my first introductions to surviving solo. I just had to get on with it. As I sat at the tiny desk in the empty cottage in Inverness, halfway up a hillside, I had the sudden realisation that, in a few days' time, I had to go on a residential course for a week and talk about personal memories in both group settings and one-to-one sessions with the course tutors. Obviously I'd have to talk about losing Richard – after all, this was a memoir course. Six weeks post bereavement, my emotions were still pretty raw. Perhaps I should've thought it through.

Moniack Mhor was located in a picturesque but isolated location on top of a hill overlooking Inverness, with Highland cows and deer in the surrounding fields. My bedroom was so small it felt like a nun's cell. It was clean and tidy but basic, with a small single bed and a desk and chair. I'm just guessing, as I've never been in a nun's bedroom, but it was about the same size as a prison cell. There was a skylight right above my bed with no blind, so I'd wake up with bright sunlight shining straight into my eyes every morning. I suddenly felt very alone and acutely aware of my loss. My life had recently been stripped of Richard and now my family and familiar possessions were also missing. What had I done?

On the first night, the group met for an evening meal to hear what was in store for us during the week. There were about 16 of us. We were being split into small groups and would each be responsible for catering for the whole group for one day of the course. That was probably in the small print that I hadn't read. I can hardly cook for myself, so catering for a large group was daunting. They gave us menus and recipes to follow, as well as all the ingredients. Thankfully, my food prep skills were up to scratch and I let the more able cooks drive our group's catering efforts. The joint activity fostered the development of relationships, which would be helpful when we were required to share personal material over the coming days.

We were given daily writing tasks and exercises, sometimes sitting out on the grass in the sunshine working on our own, then we'd come together with the tutors in a large group to share our efforts and get feedback. If I'd known it was going to be this stressful, I'd never have signed up, but as the week progressed I gradually settled into it. The two tutors were published authors and, one evening, we had a guest speaker. Some nights we'd sit around the fire pit on the side of the hill to chat and sing. On the last day we even had a piper and a Burns supper.

As the course progressed, we had writing practice sessions, exercises, sharings and individual and group feedback, plus protected time for writing our actual memoir. My imposter syndrome was alive and kicking, as there were published authors, people with creative writing degrees and journalists on the course. Doing such an intensive, immersive course six weeks after losing Richard was brave to say the least, but you learn most when you're taken out of your comfort zone, even if it leaves you feeling a bit vulnerable and wobbly. In hindsight, it was cathartic and helped me to process losing Richard, but it was in quite a public forum. On some mornings, I'd get up early and go for a walk in the countryside with one of the other authors. We'd share stories and put the world to rights. It was all part of my self-healing process and author journey. I returned from my trip having shared and processed a lot of my feelings.

I learned that memoir as a genre is quite forgiving and there aren't too many rules. You can leave in or exclude whatever you want. It's acceptable to alter names, ages and so on to maintain confidentiality, as long as you stay true to the story as you remember it. The most important technical messages for me were about the use of dialogue: avoid a lot of 'he said, she said'; use limited amounts of dialogue, but only if it adds to the plot or encapsulates a situation or emotion; show, don't tell; and if you paint an adequate picture of the scene with your words, you don't need to add 'I felt annoyed' or 'I was frustrated' – let the reader experience how you felt for themselves. I decided to use dialogue in the final chapters of I Don't Talk to Dead Bodies to convey the raw emotion of Richard's final days. Sadly, our lovely tutor Jenny lost her fight with cancer about a year later. She didn't live to see my book published, but she played a pivotal, supportive role right at the start of my author journey.

I guess being open to trying new things is less daunting when you jump in and don't overthink it. It suits my 'can do' attitude to life and extrovert personality. I've become a better person and flourished as a result, but I've been told by a more introverted friend that many of my leaps of faith might be terrifying for an introvert. That's why there's no blueprint for managing change – you need to accommodate your own preferences. However, I do believe that small tests of change that take you out of your own particular comfort zone are likely to aid forward momentum and personal growth for everyone. What would your first step be in order to move from your comfort zone or stuck position and enter into your personal stretch zone?

CHAPTER 8

Lights, camera, action...

Filling the retirement void became something of a mission as I was determined not to find myself sitting at home feeling alone and isolated. I knew myself well enough to realise that that wouldn't suit me. So I decided to fill the time as best I could until I found what really made me happy. Fraser and some of his friends had signed with a talent agency that supplied extras for film and TV, and some of them had already been extras in *Outlander*, which is filmed at studios near my home, *River City*, a Scottish TV soap opera, and even a movie. I thought, 'Why not? I'll give it a go.' When I went along to the audition, not only did I have to supply personal details and do a photoshoot, but they also took my measurements in case I needed costumes. How embarrassing! But I guessed they'd want extras who weren't all perfectly proportioned body beautifuls. Even so, seeing my dimensions written down was quite depressing.

After that, it was a waiting game until they contacted me. If I understand it correctly, a film crew contacts an agency and says 'We're looking for a middle-aged blonde woman for a TV ad, 31 May, 8 am to 3 pm', and the agency contacts all the people on their books who fit the description to ask if they're available for the designated filming slot. The bios and photos of those who are available are then sent to the producers and they make a selection. If you're chosen, you get an email booking. There were a few close calls like that, when I fitted the bill for a scene in the pub in *River City* and I was down to the last two for an insurance commercial, but sadly I missed the final cut. It appeared that young men were more in demand. Fraser's friends seemed to be in several group scenes in movies and TV shoots. Then I got an odd message asking if I was free to travel to Carlisle for a few days. I replied that I was, and it looked as if I'd been booked. However, it all seemed a bit cloak and dagger. They wouldn't say what it was for or what I'd have to do. 'Just bring an overnight bag and dark work clothes.' I had no idea what type of work they were referring to, so I assumed an office-type scene. How wrong can you be? I was told to board the train in Glasgow and I'd be met at the other end. I still had no idea what I'd be doing. All I knew was that they'd pay for my travel and hotel and I'd be getting a fee of more than £300. It was exciting but daunting at the same time as the secrecy was unusual. Maybe I was actually being recruited by MI5! I didn't have a clue.

On arrival in Carlisle, I was met by a man with a minibus, holding up a card saying 'Morrison', but he was collecting another extra as well, a small man from the west coast of Scotland. We looked like the odd couple. We were greeted warmly and whisked off to a hotel outside Carlisle. The driver said it was all top secret; he'd only been asked to collect us. So, what were we supposed to do next? 'Get your room, have dinner and you'll get a message at midnight on your phone, telling you about the schedule for tomorrow.' What a bizarre set-up. The pair of us had dinner together and I discovered the other extra was a children's entertainer. We both speculated about the task ahead and were curious about the impending midnight message. Sure enough, I received my call details.

We were being picked up just after breakfast. There were two actors and two extras involved in the filming. I was extra number one. I still didn't have a clue where we were going or what we were filming.

The minibus picked us up the next morning along with some of the crew, who'd also been staying in the hotel. It turned out we were going to a small regional airport near Carlisle, which had been taken over for a few days. We were dropped off at a hangar, where we had to go to wardrobe and makeup. It was revealed that we'd be playing the airport ground crew for an advert for the new BMW series 7. The makers of the ad were being secretive because they didn't want anyone to see the design in advance. There were security people scanning the sky in case any camera drones were flying overhead trying to get a sneak preview. We had our phones confiscated and were under oath not to take photos or reveal anything about the new car. The car itself was covered with its own fitted coat, which they zipped on and off between scenes to hide its features. It seemed as if there were camera operators, sound technicians and producers everywhere. I wore a woolly hat, blue overalls and a fleece, all of which were too tight for my big bum, despite having shared my dimensions. It wasn't my finest hour. I have no idea why we had to go to hair and makeup, because we were wearing hats and there were wind and rain machines creating an atmosphere.

We'd been instructed to walk across the edge of the airfield, in the distance, as if we were sauntering off for a lunch break. At other times, we had to stand near the door as a plane was moving slowly out of the hangar. There was a lot of repetition and hanging around – nothing too glamorous. At one point, we were told to wait inside the hangar while they filmed a scene outside, but we were there for so long that we started to think they'd forgotten about us. It was a catch-22 situation, as we debated peeking through the hangar door to shout, 'Hello, we're still here.' But they may still have been filming outside and we'd have ruined the take. And so we waited, and waited. Then a handsome young man appeared at the back of the hangar. He was one of the actors, who'd also got bored waiting. The main actor was a handsome, middle-aged silver fox from Scandinavia, but our new English friend had been hired to be the 'hand double' for the steering wheel close-ups. I'm not sure if the silver fox had gnarled claws or if they just wanted more youthful hands. Our new friend usually modelled clothes at Paris Fashion Week, so the secretive hand double gig nearer home was a novelty for him, too. The four of us had lunch together, supplied by the food truck. 'No phones' meant no sneaky selfies with the handsome actors. What a shame! It wasn't like a Hollywood film set, but still quite an experience nonetheless. Later on, when I got my phone back, I looked up the actors online. There were some very nice photos of both of them, particularly the bare-chested photos of the young hand model. I showed them to my friends when I got home. They were jealous! We headed home later that evening, never to be contacted again. You'd have thought they might've sent us a copy of the final advert. Some months later, I searched the internet to find the new BMW advert. All that money for an advert that was only a few seconds long! I didn't see any sign of the airport ground crew, so I'm assuming that we ended up on the cutting-room floor.

My next outing as an extra was a little closer to home. The email asked, 'Are you available next Sunday morning for a movie being filmed in Ayrshire, in the west of Scotland?' This time it was for a movie with a soundtrack by a British pop group. The scene was a funeral. This wasn't the best gig for the recently widowed, but there I was in a real cemetery, dressed in black, having had my hair and makeup checked in a line-up in the car park. The council workers had dug a grave and the actors were ushered to the graveside in front of us. This time it seemed more likely that we might be in the movie as we were being filmed by a huge overhead camera attached to a drone so that it could zoom into the grave as the coffin was lowered in. The top of my head might have remained in shot this time. How exciting! I've still not seen the movie. We were told there were some famous American actors in this one. Apparently one of them may have been in a Marvel film, but never having been a fan of that genre, it meant nothing to me. I'm not sure what the lady putting flowers on a grave at the other side of the cemetery made of it all.

The most entertaining part of the day was when we got to the food truck after the shoot on the hillside. We were instructed to queue up for food, but if an actor appeared we were to part like the Red Sea and let them go first. And so, despite having queued for 20 minutes to try the culinary delights, we parted, as ordered, when a young American actor swanned over from a trailer. She hadn't even been in our scene, so shouldn't have worked up much of an appetite. Suddenly, like bees around a honey pot, a group of assistant producers appeared to tend to her needs.

'What can we get you?'

'I don't know what I want, I can't decide,' said the young American in a rather pathetic, childlike voice. The staff appeared to be hanging on her every word.

'Whatever you want, we'll get it for you.'

'Do you know what I'd really like?' She paused for dramatic effect. 'I want to pat a sheep.'

This entitled wannabe fluttered her eyelashes and they were off.

'We'll make it happen... Let's get her a sheep.'

The next thing we knew, we were witnessing grown adults mobilising resources to get a sheep for the actress to pat. That's Hollywood for you. More importantly, she was keeping us from our burgers and macaroni cheese.

I recognised one of the other extras that day. He was an actor who'd starred in a musical theatre production with my son, dressed in a toga. We took a selfie together to send to

Fraser, smiling at the graveside on the hill. Fortunately, being at the mock funeral hadn't triggered too many emotions for me. However, subsequent real funerals have given me pause for thought. The lump in my throat and the tear in my eye aren't always linked to the person who's just died. More often, I've been transported back to Richard's funeral and another little piece of residual grief has slipped away.

I'm not too comfortable with showing emotions in public. For me, grief is a private emotion that bubbles to the surface and then disappears until the next time. I don't let it overwhelm me. I'm not afraid of it, but I'm its custodian and I let it out little by little when something or some situation triggers it. It can be a photograph, a discussion, a memory or a situation I'm unable to share with Richard. I guess the prospect of future weddings and grandchildren will remind me of what he'll miss. There'll be that empty chair at the table and someone absent from the photos at special occasions. Even thinking about it brings a tear to my eye, a tightness in my chest and an ache in my guts, a little more grief quietly slipping away. I still see couples for dinner with whom we used to socialise, but the table for four is now occupied by three, a constant reminder of my absent other half. It doesn't mean that I dwell on it or that I don't have a great time, but he's never far from my mind. Who knows? One day I may meet someone nice to fill the empty chair, but they'll need to be pretty special.

CHAPTER 9

Mahjong, scones and bacon rolls

I continued to make a point of trying to fill my diary with social contact and activities in the belief that I had to pick myself up and embrace life. Some other people had ideas about how to help me cope, too. I fortuitously met my friend Marion in Tesco and she told me she was off to play mahjong that evening with my friend Elaine and two other ladies. I told her that I'd had a mahjong lesson on a river cruise in China when we were celebrating my 50th birthday and had enjoyed it.

'You must come and play some time.'

'I'd like that.'

What followed was a series of invitations to join the group of ladies whenever one of the four was busy or on holiday. I gradually picked up the rules and really enjoyed the companionship, chat and mahjong itself. When it came to scoring, I left that to the experts. I also found myself being invited to weekly coffee mornings with another group of women, which included Marion and Elaine. We were a mixture of retirees and part-time professional women. The venue rotated around each

51

of our houses and it was a set menu of scones, fresh fruit, tea, coffee and chat (and for me, Irn-Bru, Scotland's famous fizzy drink!). This gave my week some friendship and structure. It was a welcome and valuable experience at such a pivotal time of transition in my life.

I made a decision to continue travelling as that had been a big part of our joint retirement plan. Here I was, planning my first solo trip with Alison and Derek. I'd decided I'd better raise my game in terms of formal wear for this five-star luxury cruise. I wanted to get some alterations done and found the business card I needed tucked into the back of my purse. When Kate came to the house to measure me and collect the dresses, we got chatting. She enquired about what I was planning to do with my retirement. I explained about Richard and how I'd returned to art and ended up with an unplanned potential small business venture. She said, 'You should come along to my business breakfast group one week and get some free advertising.'

I'm not someone who tends to do much research, so I said 'yes' quite impulsively. We made arrangements for me to attend. I had to be at a hotel in Grangemouth at silly o'clock in the morning (about 6.30 am). I didn't know it then, but the group had been declining in membership and was on the brink of folding. They welcomed me with open arms as a potential new member. It was a branch of Business Network International (BNI), which has a membership of more than 300,000 people worldwide. Each group is called a chapter, which sounds quite American. This chapter was called Turn the Music Up, and to this day I don't understand the significance. However, something clicked at that first meeting. It filled a hole that I didn't know I needed to fill.

Since losing my husband and career, I'd been sailing alone, rudderless. I no longer had a partner, a team of staff to manage, a destination, a real purpose or anything that legitimised my day-to-day activities. The tentative decision just a few months before to create Rhona Morrison Art suddenly meant a purpose was developing that legitimised my art activities. If I decided to join a business group, I'd have the weekly meeting to attend as well as some colleagues and, of course, a bacon roll for breakfast! That may have sold it. I'd have to stand up every week and talk about my business for 60 seconds, which would encourage me to get things done. I'd need to progress my plans because I'd need something to feed back to the group each week. A spark was ignited inside me... I needed this. I concluded that joining would be good for me and I liked the ethos. The idea is that you tell everyone in the room what type of referrals you're looking for each week and they effectively become your sales force. In the course of their work, whether arranging mortgages, selling fish or plumbing in a new bathroom, they look for opportunities to promote their BNI colleagues' businesses and you do the same for them in return. That involves a lot of early morning bacon rolls!

In my first week, I asked if anyone knew any cafes that might be interested in hanging and selling my art prints. The very next week, a fellow member told me he'd secured an opportunity for me with Andrew, the owner of the Corner Cafe in Falkirk. I followed up the referral and a deal was done. You don't just give someone your colleague's business card. Instead, you say that you know someone who can help them, you sing their praises, and if the person seems interested, you offer to get your colleague to call them. It means that you're not cold calling and you're also not reliant on the potential customer following up. In this instance, Andrew also kindly offered to run an evening exhibition for me. It was good PR for his cafe and for my art business. Colleagues from BNI, friends and family all supported me. I sold prints and greetings cards and even sold an original pen-and-ink drawing of the Kelpies, a local landmark. I felt as if the business was real.

My first BNI chapter folded after about six months, so I moved to the more active Building Bridges chapter. I've remained friends with Julie, the financial advisor from my first group, and she still looks after all my investments. I'm clueless but she keeps me on the right track. We always manage to fit in lunch with a financial review, which allows for gossip and a general catch-up. An unexpected benefit of joining BNI was having access to a worldwide network of professionals who can assist me personally, which is particularly helpful now that I'm on my own. I no longer have Richard to help me, but now I have Paul for plumbing, Brian for roofing, Julie for financial advice, Dave for mortgage advice and so on. Norman the handyman should've been on speed dial! Some of the names and faces have changed over the years, but there's always someone there to help.

If you're a woman living alone, trust is important. My colleagues were known to me and I trusted them. Were they the best and the cheapest? I don't know, but they were trusted friends on whom I could rely to help me. It made it easier to refer them on to my friends when I'd used them myself. My network of contacts grew outside my own chapter, so I was also known to my friends as the go-to person if they needed a tradesperson or service. My friends would say, 'Why are you getting up at 4.30 am to go to a business breakfast group every Friday morning when you've retired?' They didn't understand that it provided a much-needed anchor and structure to my week. I was going to see my friends and growing my business. The significant difference for me was that there was no pressure to make money and I could stop at any time, which was very different from paid employment in the stressful NHS. It started with a quest for cafes and shops that would sell artwork on their walls, then galleries, then invites to my open studio events and exhibitions.

I developed an entire range of merchandise for sale in shops, for example coasters, candle jars, tea towels, fine bone china mugs and greetings cards. Later, I progressed to mostly commissioned work as the shops, galleries and cafes all closed down during the pandemic. I was always out of pocket with those anyway as I had to pay to get prints made and framed, wait until they sold, and then had to give a percentage (up to 30–40 per cent) to the shop owner or gallery. It was nice to be able to say that I'd sold my artwork in the Scottish Design Exchange, but in reality it wasn't financially worthwhile and I stopped that. With commissions, I wasn't out of pocket. What satisfied me the most, though, was the fact that I was able to produce artwork with a personal meaning for the recipient and they gave me feedback. In the shops, I never knew who'd bought my work. The commissions were mostly pet portraits or wedding venues and houses, usually gifts for birthdays, anniversaries and weddings, so I honed my skills in these areas. I offered two options, either watercolour or pen-and-ink pointillism (stippling).

The more involved I became with BNI, the more I tried to embrace the ethos and give back. I worked on all the elements acknowledged to be helpful to business growth using the model of referral marketing, and reached a maximum 100 on the traffic light system used to monitor positive engagement, which is quite difficult to achieve. Colin, the director for our region, likened the process to a gym membership. You can be shown all the machines and how to work them, but if you keep paying your money and don't use the equipment, you're unlikely to get fit. BNI works for those people who use all the elements known to grow your network and develop meaningful relationships and trust. That's when the referrals come. They say you should be a farmer and not a hunter, ie cultivate relationships, support others to grow their businesses and they'll reciprocate. As a people person, the model fitted my personality. I took on the role of vice president twice, which meant more work outside the meetings, supporting the president, preparing stats for the meeting, planning events, supporting and mentoring new members, and chairing the monthly chapter success meeting. These were things that felt comfortable and meaningful to me, given my previous background. I also got to know some members better, becoming friends as a result of the increased contact. We started Spotlight sessions outside the weekly meeting, which allowed more individual input to help coach members in developing their businesses. I used some of the skills I acquired as a medical manager and business coach in the NHS, in particular the GROW (goal, reality, options, will) model we used in business coaching, developed by Sir John Whitmore and peers, which helps with goal setting, problem solving and performance improvement. It was very rewarding.

We were in lockdown when I was vice president for Dave, so we worked together mostly by Zoom and telephone. The friendship and trust we developed made it an easy decision to recommend him to Jill and Fraser as their mortgage advisor. When Paul was president and I was vice president again, we had regular weekly chats to plan, moan, scheme, gossip and so on. Often it was just a lengthy telephone chat in the car, in between Paul's latest plumbing challenges. But one Saturday, I was in the car with Jill when Paul called. I'll never forget it. 'Are you sitting down?' The message I remember after that was, 'They think Diane's brain dead.' I can't quite find the words to describe the impact of that statement. We'd been at BNI on the Friday morning. Diane, our insurance broker, had been cheery as usual and I took her photo as she was receiving an accolade of some kind. She loved the colour red. It was the colour of her company logo and she always wore red clothes. I'd ordered some red shoes on the internet the previous week, but they didn't fit. My first port of call was Diane. She had the same shoe size as me and liked them, so I'd delivered them on that Friday morning. She was heading off on holiday with her partner, Bob, later that day. I'd since received a photo of her feet in the red shoes, and here I was, a few hours later, hearing that she was probably brain dead. My head couldn't compute what I was hearing about lovely, vivacious, fun-loving Diane. It transpired that she'd had a massive intracranial bleed and subsequent cardiac arrest in a hotel in London prior to flying off on holiday. She'd been taken to hospital and was on life support. They were going to carry out tests over the next couple of days, but they thought that she was brain dead.

Over the next few months, Paul and I found ourselves navigating a difficult path, trying to manage the grief of the group members and support Bob, her family and colleagues impacted by Diane's sudden illness and subsequent death. Paul was an absolute star, going above and beyond his role, to steer all of us through that phase. Sometimes people shine in times of adversity. Paul was one of those people.

CHAPTER 10

The pest controller

Within BNI, you agree to turn up every week or provide a substitute in your place. That's a challenge when you're asking a colleague or friend to travel a distance to a meeting at 6.45 am. Why is it necessary? Because each member pays a substantial fee and commits to actively seek referrals for other members. If you don't attend, you don't hear their 60-second pitch and what they're looking for, so they're short changed. You also don't get to deliver your own 60-second pitch to remind people of the kind of referrals you're looking for. If a substitute attends, even if it's your granny who doesn't have a business, they'll read out your 60-second pitch and hear everyone else's. They're a potential customer themselves, with their own network, so may be able to pass referrals or recommend businesses to their friends.

I was advised that it would be good to 'sub' at other chapters to grow my network. As there were no other artists in our region, I was likely to pick up some referrals after people got to know me and saw some examples of my work, so I regularly took something with me. When you're subbing for someone, you get a chance to do your own 60-second pitch too, assuming you aren't in a clashing category with any of their members. As usual, I stood up and said that I was a retired consultant forensic psychiatrist turned artist and was looking for referrals to cafes or shops that might be willing to hang or sell my framed prints. I also showed a print of my watercolour painting of the Old Course golf course at St Andrews, which featured the famous Swilken Bridge. I wondered if anyone knew someone who worked at the hotel shop and might be able to get me an introduction to sell my prints there. The sub sitting next to me was called Ray. He was a pest controller. On the surface we had nothing in common, but BNI is all about networking. We exchanged business cards, as you do. I wasn't expecting to see him again. How wrong can you be? A few days later, a text message arrived from Ray. 'I know someone who manages the tearoom at the Old Course Hotel. I've messaged her for you about the paintings.' So, someone had been listening to my 60-second pitch. I thanked him, not expecting anything to come of it. A few days later, another text message arrived. 'I was at the gun club last night. The man from the community council was there. I asked him about cafes and he named two that didn't have anything on the wall. I've popped in to see them; they're keen and expecting your call. Here are the contact details.' Well, I wasn't expecting that! I thanked him and made arrangements to visit the cafes. Both eventually took my framed prints to sell. I was delighted.

A few days later, I received another message from Ray. 'Have you ever painted Dalgety Bay? You should, it's lovely. Are you free on Monday? Come to mine and we'll give you a plate of soup then take the dog for a walk and show you our favourite spot.' I accepted the pest controller's invitation. When I returned home from my day out in Dalgety Bay, I selected my favourite photograph and started a painting. A few days later, it was me who sent a text including a photo of the painting. I'm a quick worker. Ray liked it and wanted to buy it, so I went on another trip to Dalgety Bay to deliver it.

This whole chain of events and referrals came from a chance meeting of two subs at a BNI meeting who, on the surface, had little in common. This is an example of serendipity, where good luck comes from an unexpected, fortunate interaction with a stranger. The chain reaction happened when I took up the initial opportunity. It would be the first of many serendipitous events along the way. Ray had nothing to gain by making all these introductions, feeding me soup, taking me around Dalgety Bay and buying a painting. He was demonstrating 'giver's gain', the ethos of BNI. I didn't have a rat infestation or a mouse in the cupboard, so I couldn't reciprocate at that point. However, his kind actions stayed with me. The kindness of strangers always remains in my mind.

Sometime later, at an art festival, a lady spoke to me about her artwork. I told her that I'd built a studio in my garden and she told me she lived on a farm and had set up a studio in her barn. She'd been unwell and hadn't painted recently. As a result, there were now rats in the barn. I seized my chance. 'Do you need a pest controller? I know a really good one.' She nodded. 'I can contact him right now with your details and get him to call you if you like.' I did, and Ray got the job.

Months later, squirrels built a nest in my attic. They were rampaging about in tackety boots (in England, they're called hobnailed boots). Well, it sounded like that. I thought, I know a good pest controller. Apparently, squirrels don't like music or lights, so I had a squirrel disco, with flashing strobe lights and a radio on in my loft 24/7 until we eventually got rid of them. We needed poison and a trap, too. I dread the thought of their return. This whole story would be replicated in different forms over the next five years at BNI, with different members. Paul, the plumbing and gas engineer, came to my book launch, bought a book for himself, then bought several other books for friends, and also left one abroad and one in the community 'help yourself' library phone box. He introduced me to the local radio station host, Jimmy Rainbow, who did an interview with me live on air. It was recorded and broadcast from a tiny, home-based radio station. A kids' programme was on just before me. It was an interesting segue from 'the wheels on the bus go round and round' to discussing mentally ill murderers and sex offenders, but there we are. Jimmy unashamedly plugged my book. Paul then told me one of his other friends hosts a podcast about mental health, so he introduced me to Cuddy, who interviewed me for his podcast, then introduced me to his friend in London for another podcast.

Paul also contacted the local library in Dalgety Bay to try to secure me a Meet the Author event. He was told he'd need to speak to the book club. This required him to join the book club, to access their Facebook page. Undeterred, he did that and got me a slot. The night before the talk, he decided to advertise it on the local area community Facebook page. Then he turned up at the talk (the only man who came to support me). Two criminology lecturers from the local college had seen the Facebook post and turned up as well. This resulted in the sale of several books on the day and a booking to speak at the college, which subsequently resulted in multiple book sales. About 25 students all queued up to buy a signed copy following my talk. After the library talk, Paul's wife Jennifer made lunch for us. That's not a business acquaintance from a business breakfast group – that's a friend! One night, the three of us went to a fancy-dress birthday party, Jennifer as Jessie and Paul as Woody (from *Toy Story*) on an inflatable horse, and me as the singer Boy George – quite the trio! They invited me to their house first, which was thoughtful, as it meant I didn't have to arrive on my own. However, the trip there in my car, dressed as Boy George, was awkward, especially when I stopped at traffic lights and the people in the next car stared at me!

Sam was the treasurer when I was on the leadership team. What a committed young man. He worked for Teens+ charity, which supports young people transitioning from school who have additional support needs. If anyone embodies a positive, inclusive, non-discriminatory culture, it's Sam. We became friends, particularly as I have a long-standing experience with a similar client group, and because my sister Vivienne had a learning disability, physical disability and sensory impairment. Visiting this charity was always heartwarming. There are still good, committed people out there. We'd regularly fundraise within the BNI chapter to support the charity. Sam dressed in drag for our murder mystery party as we were short of female characters. This was quite a sight to behold. Once seen, never forgotten: wig, mini skirt, hairy legs and ladies' sandals!

CHAPTER 11

Rotary in action

Despite all my activities with BNI, there was still something lacking in my life. I'd spent my entire career helping and caring for people and now there were no patients to assist. It felt really selfish to be able to do whatever I wanted for the rest of my life. I was discussing this with Dot, my picture framer friend, who suggested I come along to her Rotary Club in Kilsyth to see if joining this organisation might fill that gap. I'd already persuaded her to join BNI. I found out that Rotary is an international service organisation with more than a million members worldwide. They engage in service projects and charitable fundraising to help local communities, charities and global initiatives to enhance lives. I went along to one meeting and decided to join right away. It fulfilled the 'caring for others' element that was missing from my life. Sadly, just a few months later, fundraising ended abruptly as we entered the first lockdown of the pandemic. (You can find out more about how my Covid journey began in Chapter 15.) The future seemed scary and uncertain. We were entering Zoom Rotary territory.

I'd managed to work out that the club had several committees – community/vocational, international/foundation, club service and youth – and I'd been allocated to club service, which is essentially the social committee for local club events. Fellowship is a huge part of Rotary – it builds relationships, friendships and keeps people engaged. This was going to be a challenge, but as my mind constantly generates ideas, it was quite invigorating for me. Now I had the challenge of coming up with some inventive 'Covid-safe' ideas. It was important to keep everyone engaged in terms of managing their social isolation and mental health. We ended up running a series of really successful social events and even managed some fundraising. People were still allowed to walk their dogs, so we held a 'Bandanarama' dog walk. We bought chequered bandanas for the dogs and attached small Rotary badges to them. People purchased one for £10 and took their dog for a walk wearing it. They had to submit a cute photo of their dog wearing the bandana to be in with a chance of winning a pet portrait by Rhona Morrison Art. I picked the cutest photo, painted it, and Dot framed it. We made about £9 profit per entry, and all of it went to charitable causes. After the pandemic, we ran a successful in-person Bandanarama event down on the canal walkway, and it may become an annual event.

Isolation was such a problem, especially for some of our older members, that we decided on an event where people didn't need to leave their homes. My new Rotary friend Elaine and I did some home baking and made up afternoon tea boxes, then delivered them to everyone's doorstep. In the afternoon, we all went online for a virtual afternoon tea and bingo session. I accidentally ordered two bingo sets, so donated one to Sam's Teens+ charity. When people were able to travel a bit further, we decided on a car treasure hunt. I made up the route and clues, which could mostly be spotted from the car window. Only occasionally did one person have to pop out to read a noticeboard for extra clues. Elaine and I made goody bags of home baking for each carload of people. We ended up back at our own homes and went online for a Zoom social to share the answers. One of the participants had undergone a liver transplant and, because of immunosuppression, had to be particularly careful about self-isolation. It was such a triumph to know we'd come up with a social event that even she could enjoy from the passenger seat of the car, wearing a mask.

Following a BNI visit from an expert from the gin distillery on the Isle of Bute, I decided to hold a Rotary Zoom gin tasting. We distributed the packs in advance so that everyone had all the little gin samples, mixers and herbs required as they were guided through the tasting by the experts from the distillery. Who knew that oyster gin would be so popular?

When my children were younger they used to enjoy dressing up. One time we took Fraser to a *Sound of Music* singalong event dressed as a brown paper package tied up with string. When the host shouted out 'Do we have any nuns in tonight?', the lady next to me, who was dressed as a grassy mountain covered with edelweiss, put her hand up. She turned to me and said, 'I'm a real nun, but I thought that was a bit boring!' The kids used to have murder mystery birthday parties too, so I'd wondered whether something like that would work online. I trialled one with my BNI colleagues and then with former colleagues from the forensic team, and they worked really well. Everyone came online dressed as their character. We'd sent them their character booklet in advance, so we were good to go. I decided to use the idea at Rotary as a Zoom social. What a laugh we had! We ended up doing it twice as it was such good fun. A note for anyone who has never done one: really go for it with the costumes and makeup as it's so much funnier if you do. If you can throw in a French accent, a limp, don a wig and really embrace the character, you'll get so much more from the experience.

After Covid restrictions were lifted, we held a follow-up murder mystery event at the local golf club. I turned up in the car park dressed as a pirate in ragged cut-off trousers, long stripy socks, a long black wig, a moustache and a pirate captain's hat, with a stuffed parrot on my shoulder. I must've been quite a sight, emerging from my car with a sword, hook and a box of home baking as golfers were taking their clubs out of the boots of their cars.

I'm particularly proud of one fundraising idea I came up with. End Polio Now is Rotary International's project aimed at eradicating polio throughout the world. Rotary launched Polio Plus in 1985, and so far more than 2.5 billion children have had the vaccine. The world is currently 99 per cent polio free. Every year, each club is challenged with making a contribution to End Polio Now. Our club usually aims to send £1,500 per year, but how were we going to raise that amount during lockdown? I knew that this awareness-raising programme was linked to the Purple4Polio campaign. In developing countries where vaccination programmes are active, the system for medical records, especially in rural communities, is often poor and records are scant. When the project is underway, they use purple dye to paint the pinkies of those who have been vaccinated in order that they can be identified. Over in the UK, we sell purple crocus pin badges, plant purple crocuses and illuminate local buildings purple to raise awareness about the initiative.

I decided to start the 'Message of Hope' campaign. As a psychiatrist, I was worried about the impact of social isolation, illness and bereavement on people's mental health during the pandemic. As a Rotary volunteer, I worried that the End Polio Now programme would falter without funding. My solution? Design a blank greetings card featuring a pointillism crocus plant and splodges of purple dye on the front and a message about End Polio Now on the back, with a purple envelope. If we encouraged people to buy cards and send them to people impacted by the problems connected with Covid isolation, we'd be sending a Message of Hope to let them know they hadn't been forgotten, and send the profits to fund End Polio Now. The cards were sold in packs of five for £10, which gave us £7.50 profit per pack. Philanthropist Bill Gates supports Rotary's End Polio Now project and pledged to donate £2 for every £1 we raised. We sold lots of cards, then tea towels with the same image. Having made £3,000 profit, we were able to exceed previous donations, and this then multiplied to £9,000 due to the contribution from the Bill Gates Foundation.

I was honoured to become club president for the Rotary year 2022–3, particularly as I was still fairly new to Rotary. The following year, while I was attending our annual Taste of Burns Night (in memory of the famous Scottish poet Robert Burns), I was surprised and humbled to be awarded a Paul Harris Fellowship and receive a Rotary citation for my year as president. I was informed that my achievement with the Message of Hope campaign was part of the reason for that accolade. My friend Elaine had invited Jill, Fraser and Alisa to the Burns Supper and, much to my surprise, they'd agreed to attend. It later became clear why they were there – to see Mum receive her surprise award.

It was a great pleasure to be able to return the favour to Elaine when the club had its 50th anniversary charter dinner. We'd spent months planning the celebration event, but unfortunately I was going to miss the big night as I was on a cruise. Our president, Janice, approached me in advance to say that Elaine had been nominated for a Paul Harris award and would I do the surprise announcement on the night? I was going to be somewhere near Guatemala at that point, but obviously I wanted to do it for my friend, so I agreed to make a video to be shown on the night. Elaine and I have now become really good friends and often meet up at the local garden centre for a catch-up to hatch our next fundraising idea or plan who's making which home-baked item for the next event. Of course, as fellow cruise enthusiasts, there's often a bit of travel gossip to be had too.

In the 2023–4 Rotary year, I became convener for the youth committee and the aim was for Rotary to re-engage with local schools after the pandemic. One of the main achievements was supporting fellow Rotarian Janice with the introduction of Rotakids Clubs in two local primary schools. In 2024–25, my role changed to convener for the international/foundation committee. So, in addition to supporting our usual End Polio Now fundraising efforts and humanitarian initiatives for developing countries and disaster zones, we've been working on a collaboration with the Uphill Trust to raise £4,500 to build a vocational training classroom in Uphill School in rural Uganda. My initial contact with Belinda from the charity came via BNI. We raised a large proportion of the money with club initiatives such as an international quiz night, wine tasting, comical crocheted creations (funny hats for cats) and an alphabet quiz, plus we were awarded a Rotary district grant. This was enhanced by the charity's own fundraising and donations from other Rotary Clubs and individuals. I'm incredibly proud to say that we hit the target and will watch the development with interest. Perhaps there will be more foreign travel in my future to see the classroom and meet the children. Never say never!

We also committed to designing worksheets for a new Rotary badge for young people to introduce them to the seven areas of focus within Rotary and the idea of giving service to help others. The previous year we'd encouraged local people to knit hats for babies in Ukraine and I had designed a greetings card that we sold to raise money. It featured a watercolour painting of Ukraine's national flower, the sunflower, and came in a blue envelope, as yellow and blue are the colours of the Ukrainian flag. Unfortunately, there was no Bill Gates multiplier this time but we were proud of what we achieved. It's fun being able to use local people's skills for the benefit of others.

CHAPTER 12

Is it just me?

When I was a medical leader, I took part in a Myers-Briggs personality test that was aimed at giving me a greater self-awareness regarding my strengths and weaknesses, how these traits might impact my leadership style and how I relate to others. There isn't a good or a bad result, as all sorts of people are needed to make a rounded team. It just gives you a better idea of what people need to function at their best and how your behaviour may negatively impact others. For example, if you're an extrovert running a brainstorming session, you should provide prior notice of the topic and reference reading materials in advance for those more reflective introverts who need time and space to consider the information and formulate their thoughts before being asked to contribute, in the moment, by someone who thinks aloud while they're talking (like me!). I can't claim to have totally nailed that practice, due to the fast pace and volume of work in the NHS, but hopefully it's a top tip to get the best out of all team members. The extroverts probably won't have opened the email with any pre-read materials, so you need to cover all bases. They may have been too busy socialising with friends the night before!

It struck me that knowing your personality type can be really helpful in times of transition. So, how can you recognise an extrovert? They like working in groups, enjoy trying new things, are often described by others as energetic, prefer talking through their problems, make friends easily and can be quite impulsive. I chose to work in a multidisciplinary clinical team and also led the service improvement team as I enjoyed service development. I'm a multitasker. I think aloud and formulate ideas as I talk; I enjoy meeting new people and am happy to jump in and try something new. Extroverts gain energy from social interactions and too much alone time drains them of energy, resulting in them feeling listless. As an ideas person, I was always happy to write a proposal or strategy from scratch because there was an empty page that needed to be filled, but would cope less well with making several amended versions of a document or commenting on someone else's work as this wasn't energising for me. I also struggled to work directly with colleagues who were slow, pedantic and detail focused, as I'd feel bored and frustrated with the lack of progress. I appreciated the quality of their contributions in the end, but struggled with the journey to get there as I prefer bouncing ideas off colleagues to researching them. That's why we have teams of people who all bring different skills to the table.

Extroverts would much rather be the centre of attention, rarely turn down an invitation to socialise, feel comfortable in unfamiliar situations, enjoy events where they can meet total strangers and feel comfortable striking up a conversation with them. I seek out opportunities to socialise and talk and prefer a full diary. I love going out with friends and meeting interesting new people. Extroverts are also adaptable and often spontaneous decision makers. I thoroughly enjoy brainstorming and being challenged to find a solution to a problem when the parameters have changed. The pros to this personality type are that extroverts excel at making social connections, often have well-developed social skills and enjoy discussing topics and being expressive, so they may also excel at public speaking. The cons are that extroverts have difficulty dealing with extended periods of isolation and may fail to think before they speak. Their tendency to dominate conversations may make it more difficult for them to listen. So, if I were to compare myself to that description, I'd say that I categorically fall into the extrovert end of the spectrum. The best way to demonstrate this would be to simply share my diary activity in a typical week:

* Saturday: Shopping with Jill then lunch. Collect Mum to see Fraser's musical theatre production.
* Sunday: Visit Mum and do her shopping. Social media posts x 2 for tomorrow. Catch up with Morag.
* Monday: Work on art commission pet portrait.
* Tuesday: Meet Alison for lunch at the garden centre. Finish pet portrait.
* Wednesday: Visit Mum and take her out for lunch. Take the pet portrait to the gallery for framing.
* Thursday: Rotary Club meeting (visitor host for guest speaker). Prepare stats for the BNI meeting on Friday.
* Friday: BNI meeting followed by chapter success meeting. Meal with Lynn and Gillies at Nonna's Kitchen.

In summary, this was a fairly typical week with quite a bit of socialising and not a lot of downtime. I'm not exhausted and in need of sleep at the end of a week like this – in fact, I usually feel invigorated. My family and friends worry about me and say 'You should take some time to relax', but if I sit doing nothing, I feel as if someone has taken out my batteries. However, I've discovered that I can relax and switch off by watching really naff Hallmark movies (romantic or Christmas ones, at any time of the year). I stumbled upon them one Christmas when I was overloaded at work. I was doing my own full-time job as a consultant forensic psychiatrist and associate medical director for mental health services. In addition, I was acting general manager for multiple services for 12 months. My working day was 5.45 am to midnight on most days, interspersed with the school run, homework and extracurricular duties as a taxi mum. I was just about coping, juggling all the balls during the day, but I was mentally and physically exhausted. I needed some alone time to switch off from all responsibilities and not communicate with anyone. I'd retreat to our spare lounge and just sit in front of the TV and watch inane movies about Christmas tree lots, decorating Christmas cookies and winter festivals. The main characters would always fall in love, kiss under some mistletoe, the end. There was no need to follow a plot, no intrigue or suspense, no scary soundtrack. They always lived happily ever after. There was no stress or cognitive engagement required. This wasn't the most intellectually stimulating pursuit, but it worked for me. I was relieved to discover some years later that my cruise buddy Frances, a psychologist, uses exactly the same Hallmark film strategy to chill out. So, even this self-proclaimed extrovert has her limits and recognises the benefits of time to recharge. When I'm busy, I now actively seek out these films in the evening before bed to relax. They actually have their own dedicated channel, so I'm not alone.

When I was working, it took being rushed to hospital with central chest pain for me to say 'Enough is enough' and tell my employer that I'd no longer be covering the general manager post on top of everything else. Fortunately, it wasn't a heart attack, but subsequent investigations revealed that I do appear to have multiple small gallstones. Lucky me!

I'd definitely say that my extroverted personality traits have become more exaggerated in retirement as I no longer have the modifying influences of my role as a senior doctor and medical manager or my more conservative, less extroverted husband. Richard used to enjoy sitting as a couple for dinner, playing on his iPad and watching the waves go by when we were cruising and would happily not have disembarked at ports. I compromised by sitting on our own for dinner and, as a result, we hardly ever met people on the cruise ship, but Richard compromised by going on all the port excursions with me. Later, we had to curtail the excursions too, as they would become too tiring for Richard. Travelling solo as a retired person, free of these constraints and compromises, has been liberating. I embrace shared dining, meeting new people, chatting in queues and benefiting from the interesting and unexpected long-term connections that these behaviours generate.

It was analytical psychologist Carl Jung who originally coined the terms introvert and extrovert to describe how different people have different attitudes and ways of directing their energy. So how can you recognise an introvert? They're more likely to enjoy alone time, prefer independent work, tend to consider things carefully, are creative and naturally good listeners. They're typically more focused on their internal thoughts and feelings and expend energy when spending time with others. Being around large groups of people can leave them feeling drained. However, they may become excellent public speakers, thoroughly researching and preparing their content in advance, but may experience a sort of hangover fatigue afterwards. In contrast, extroverts will feel energised by the same social situation, while the introverts will need time alone to recharge. Solitary hobbies such as reading and gardening may be popular with introverts, as they provide some alone time and peace and quiet. Being internally focused means they need time to reflect and may be described as quiet or shy. In fact, they may not be shy at all, but they're more likely to have a small group of close friends, so they may be 'selectively social' rather than 'antisocial'. They may just prefer to avoid large groups of strangers.

There's nothing wrong with preferring your own company and choosing to socialise with a small group of close friends. It only becomes a problem if you actively avoid social activity in order to avoid the resulting exhaustion, as this may result in feelings of loneliness, isolation or feeling left out. I don't tend to have this type of problem, but this doesn't mean that I always feel comfortable in social situations. I don't drink alcohol because I don't particularly like the taste. And I don't like being around people when they're intoxicated. I'm also a bit of a control freak, so I don't like the idea of alcohol impacting my behaviour.

I've also witnessed the devastating impact of alcohol-fuelled violence while working in prisons, so that has no doubt played its part in my decision to be a non-drinker. Fortunately, I don't feel the need for alcohol to loosen me up in order to function socially as some people do. I'm happy to order soft drinks and don't feel social pressure to conform, but I struggle to know when and how to extricate myself from a situation when others around me are getting more than a little tipsy. When you're sober, the jokes aren't quite as funny and it's hard to erase what you've seen an inebriated colleague get up to, particularly if they've been inappropriately amorous with someone else when they're married. Their credibility as a professional person, my respect for them and my trust in their ability to be discreet have been dented. What might they say or do when not totally in control of their behaviour next time? During work nights out, I never booked a room to stay over and always left by midnight, hoping to miss any late-night shenanigans. Colleagues are more likely to relax after the boss has left.

There are several tips to assist introverts if they feel socially anxious but would like to make more friends. As with all things, these are a pick and mix of ideas from which to choose whatever suits each unique individual. It may be useful to build on existing hobbies and interests. For example, if you like reading, consider joining a book club as you already have a shared interest with other group members and this could subsequently lead to more meaningful connections. Reconnecting with old friends avoids the 'getting to know you' introduction stage. If face-to-face interactions with strangers feel too daunting, perhaps join an online forum, where you have similar interests but you get a chance to consider responses before replying and therefore there's less pressure to perform in the moment.

You could always befriend an extrovert and take them with you to social situations, which might take the pressure off if you feel exhausted by socialising. When you meet new people, try some questions that shine the spotlight on them and get them talking. Just be curious. When it comes to social interactions, quality is better than quantity. Remember to pace yourself and build in alone time before and after socialising to recharge your energy. If you feel exhausted during a social interaction, you could always excuse yourself for a toilet break or offer to help in the kitchen, just to take care of your own energy levels. Setting small, achievable goals is a good idea. For example, accept an invitation to coffee once a month (if you've previously avoided it), or go to the theatre on your own, but challenge yourself to chat to the stranger sitting next to you during the interval, to ask if they're enjoying the show.

Small challenges that take you outside your comfort zone may feel less daunting than some of the 'crazy' decisions I've gone on to make. Interestingly, when I discussed this with my editor, Bev, who's more of an introvert, she said that she sometimes finds social situations with people she doesn't know really awkward, but if she's wearing a particular 'hat' she can perform in that role. For example, she can host an event, sing in a band and used to interview musicians all over the world when she was a rock journalist. Interestingly, she did one of the first interviews with Spandau Ballet and is credited with coining the term 'New Romantics'. Despite our personality differences, I can relate to the 'it's easier performing in a hat' idea. I also feel more comfortable performing tasks when I'm wearing a particular hat. In some way, when I've been given a hat or role, it feels as if I've also been given permission and authority to perform that role, so I feel more confident. Actors often develop more confidence when inhabiting a different character. I wonder if that feels familiar and where you'd put yourself on the introvert–extrovert spectrum. Wherever that may be, it will undoubtedly affect the way in which you navigate change.

However, don't ever try to become something you're not. What you should be trying to do is look after yourself and improve your wellbeing, which may include working towards feeling a bit more connected, but it may not. Some chief executives I've known are natural introverts but can command a room by performing in their hat if required. It's an acquired skill rather than a natural personality trait. Occasionally introverts with significant social anxiety may need to seek input from a therapist or executive coach, and this can be a safe place to discuss new strategies, learn and practise new social skills. Hopefully, my tales and reflections of being an extrovert solo traveller will entertain but also inspire some of you to step out of your comfort zone and try something new in your stretch zone, but in your own unique way.

Chapter 13

Cuddly koalas and Texan quizzers

I needed something smarter for my luxury cruise with Alison and Derek, so I bought new suitcases for my first solo trip. We were flying business class, which was another first for me. What a bizarre experience that was. I was in the window seat pod and Alison was beside me in the aisle pod as she anticipated needing to get up to stretch her legs. As we hit the overnight leg of the flight, I put my seat into the bed position, put my blankets and pillow in place and dozed off. I woke up in the middle of the dark cabin, needing to use the toilet, so I put my seat back into the sitting position. Houston, we have a problem! There appeared to be no way of making my way to the aisle. All the pods were full of people stretched out, asleep. I thought it must've been me, that I was missing something obvious. I stood in the dark for a while, eventually attracting the steward's attention.

'How do I get to the toilet?'

'Just climb over that man's bed.'

Really? I was expected to straddle the bed of a sleeping

I needed something smarter for my luxury cruise with Alison and Derek, so I bought new suitcases for my first solo trip. We were flying business class, which was another first for me. What a bizarre experience that was. I was in the window seat pod and Alison was beside me in the aisle pod as she anticipated needing to get up to stretch her legs. As we hit the overnight leg of the flight, I put my seat into the bed position, put my blankets and pillow in place and dozed off. I woke up in the middle of the dark cabin, needing to use the toilet, so I put my seat back into the sitting position. Houston, we have a problem! There appeared to be no way of making my way to the aisle. All the pods were full of people stretched out, asleep. I thought it must've been me, that I was missing something obvious. I stood in the dark for a while, eventually attracting the steward's attention.

'How do I get to the toilet?'

'Just climb over that man's bed.'

Really? I was expected to straddle the bed of a sleeping

Chapter 13

Cuddly koalas and Texan quizzers

I needed something smarter for my luxury cruise with Alison and Derek, so I bought new suitcases for my first solo trip. We were flying business class, which was another first for me. What a bizarre experience that was. I was in the window seat pod and Alison was beside me in the aisle pod as she anticipated needing to get up to stretch her legs. As we hit the overnight leg of the flight, I put my seat into the bed position, put my blankets and pillow in place and dozed off. I woke up in the middle of the dark cabin, needing to use the toilet, so I put my seat back into the sitting position. Houston, we have a problem! There appeared to be no way of making my way to the aisle. All the pods were full of people stretched out, asleep. I thought it must've been me, that I was missing something obvious. I stood in the dark for a while, eventually attracting the steward's attention.

'How do I get to the toilet?'

'Just climb over that man's bed.'

Really? I was expected to straddle the bed of a sleeping

stranger in the dark, trying not to disturb him? He woke up just as I got my leg over and smiled up at me. I was mortified. I'd paid a fortune to travel business class, but this wasn't dignified. This next statement will seem sexist, but the designer of this cabin had to be a man. No woman would've designed it like that. Imagine if someone who'd been sexually abused in the past woke up in an unfamiliar environment and found a strange man straddling them in the dark. That would be traumatic.

We eventually arrived in Singapore, our first stop for a few days. My luggage failed to appear. Everyone else had left the carousel and we were still waiting. Disaster! After a protracted wait, my battered and broken suitcase finally emerged. It was too damaged to be repaired, so I'd need to buy a new one in Singapore. Our stress levels were heightened as we'd been invited to join Derek for the New Year celebrations at the Singapore branch of his company. As he was the CEO, we were guests of honour. After a quick change, we were off to a lavish reception and some bonkers karaoke.

The plan over the next few days was to visit several tourist spots in Singapore, including a walk around the harbour to see the Merlion fountain, a trip to the Gardens by the Bay with its huge metal trees and botanical gardens, a river cruise and a trip to Raffles for a Singapore Sling. We achieved all our goals, but I opted out of a game of badminton in the evening with Derek's colleagues as I was having a full-blown meltdown in my hotel room. It was all my own fault. We had to apply for a visa to enter Australia, so I'd filled out an online form. Derek and Alison had theirs granted almost immediately but mine hadn't come through by the time we left the UK. I was getting increasingly anxious as the flight to Australia drew closer. At this point, Derek enlisted his company lawyer to assist me. She was lovely and took me to the Australian embassy. We arrived at the gatehouse but the man on duty refused us entry. We explained that it was urgent; I was due to fly to Australia in two days' time and needed to speak to someone. He told us to send an email, handing the lawyer a tiny strip of paper indicating the address. She calmly escorted me back to the hotel and emailed an urgent message, stating her position and my predicament. I was both frustrated and distraught. Was I going to be stranded in Singapore on my own? I couldn't spoil Derek and Alison's big holiday. They'd have to go on without me. If Richard were here, he'd know what to do. At that moment, I felt vulnerable and alone, way out of my comfort zone. This was my first real solo holiday wake-up call. I'd always depended on Richard for practical organisational tasks as that was his forte.

The situation appeared to be of my own making. I'd watched TV programmes about border control in Australia and how strict they are. If you answer a question falsely, you're taken into a small room for questioning and often refused entry. So, when it came to the question on the visa application form about any previous convictions, I thought I'd better confess to a speeding fine for doing 40 mph in a 30 mph zone years ago. Apparently that doesn't count as a conviction, but what did I know? Anyway, when you tick 'no' to everything, I suspect it goes straight into an electronic pile for the automatic issuance of a visa. But if you highlight any issues like I did, you get put onto a human action pile. Unfortunately, I didn't know it was a holiday weekend in Australia (for Australia Day), so my application hadn't been processed.

While I was crying myself to sleep, Derek was secretly contacting his travel agent back home trying to work out how to sort out my flights if the visa didn't come through in time. He'd also contacted the hotel management to ensure I could extend my stay if necessary. Unfortunately, all the business class flights were linked, so if I didn't use the one I'd booked to Australia, I'd need to rebook and pay for new ones. My first trip travelling solo was turning out to be quite stressful. Derek kindly omitted to tell me about the linked flights as I was already in bits. But after all that, I woke early the next morning to find an email confirming that my visa had been approved. I was so relieved! Despite my emotional meltdown, Singapore left a really good impression on me as a safe, clean place with lots to see and do. After purchasing and packing my new suitcase, we were off to Australia.

We'd be spending a few days in Sydney, where we certainly packed in a lot. I cuddled a koala at a small city zoo, ate at a beachfront restaurant at sunset, climbed the iconic Sydney Harbour Bridge with Derek and went to see *La Bohème* with Alison at the Sydney Opera House. It was soon time to board my first five-star luxury cruise, meet my butler, relax and be looked after, as we took a tour around New Zealand. But first, a trip to Melbourne for a scenic trip on a vintage steam train to see a kookaburra and white cockatoos.

In the course of the two-week cruise, I visited kangaroos in the wild and tried boomerang throwing, visited the geysers and hot springs at Rotorua, enjoyed unspoilt Stewart Island and picturesque Milford Sound, took a trip to a penguin sanctuary and an albatross colony in Dunedin, went to a vineyard for a wine tasting, watched a farmer shearing a sheep on a ranch, walked around an arboretum, went on a Jeep safari over the mountains, enjoyed a speedboat adventure, found out about Maori traditional wood carving and facial tattoos, indulged in fine dining, sipped mocktails and experienced five-star service at its best. One night, we even cooked our own food on a hot lava stone out on deck.

Dunedin made an impact on me for several reasons. I spent a month there in the mid-1980s for my university elective, studying services for learning disability psychiatry, so I had lots of fond memories of the place. When we were visiting the albatross colony at the top of the mountain, I bumped into my tennis partner and her husband from Cumbernauld. What are the chances? I couldn't even stop to talk as I was on an excursion and didn't want to lose my tour guide. We took a quick selfie in the gift shop and I was off again.

People often talk about the beauty of Milford Sound. It

was beautiful, but I found myself thinking, 'We have beautiful scenery like this in Scotland.' I sometimes forget just how fortunate we are in Scotland. Visiting the Maori meeting house in Rotorua and seeing all the costumes took me back to my visit to the Maori museum when I was a medical student all those years ago. I was definitely on a trip down memory lane, although last time I was living in hospital accommodation with a shared bathroom and canteen food!

The entertainment on the ship was excellent, and every afternoon people played team trivia. On the first day, I declined to join a team with Derek and Alison as I hate quizzes, but I wandered down to watch from the sidelines while reading my book. However, that plan lasted about five minutes until four Texans adopted me – Karen, Jimmy, Richard and Gail. I contributed virtually nothing to the team's endeavours but made some good friends. We met every day to see if we could surpass the score from the day before. We were never going to be winners, but that didn't matter. At the end of the cruise, Karen and I exchanged email addresses and she promised to keep in touch. I didn't really think she would. How wrong can you be?

Although we were sad to disembark after two weeks, we were excited as we still had another two weeks of travelling to go. We disembarked in Auckland, and after spending some time there, we hired a car and drove up to the Bay of Islands on the North Island before flying to Hong Kong for a few days. We had a lovely time travelling around New Zealand in the car. Away from the cities, it's quiet, clean and unspoilt. Hong Kong, on the other hand, was built up, busy and culturally very different. We were all pretty exhausted by this point but we visited Hong Kong Gardens and took the tram up to the Peak, the highest viewpoint, for a spectacular panoramic view over Hong Kong Island and Kowloon Peninsula. We took the Star Ferry across the bay between Hong Kong Island and Kowloon as we watched the famous light display on the buildings in Hong Kong harbour before having a feast in a restaurant overlooking the bay.

I love aromatic crispy duck and chose that for my main course, but Alison and Derek fancied trying it as our starter, so I ordered an alternative main. What I thought I'd ordered was chicken with a sweet chilli sauce. What I actually ordered was something that was photo-worthy for all the wrong reasons. Chilli chicken was, in fact, a plate full of very hot red chillies with a couple of pieces of chicken chopped up in it for garnish. It was so hot that I couldn't eat it, but I have the photographic evidence! One thing I wouldn't recommend, however, is going on the underground MTR (Mass Transit Railway). It certainly carries the masses, but 'sardines' doesn't begin to describe how closely packed we were on that train. If you fainted, you'd still be standing upright for the whole journey, wedged between all the other passengers.

After four and a half weeks, we were ready to return home from our adventure. Alison and Derek were so generous to have shared this special trip with me and include a little taste of the Far East to replace the retirement cruise with Richard that had to be cancelled. What did I learn? That I could continue this cruising malarkey all on my own, because Karen and Jimmy showed me that people are kind and inclusive when they recognise you're a solo traveller, but you have to put yourself out there, talk to people and join in. I thought, 'I can do that.'

I like five-star cruising because the level of service is exemplary and I don't feel as lost as I might do on a huge ship. It's small and personal and I feel I'll be looked after and not forgotten. Bizarrely, I also randomly discovered something about myself that surprised me. Apparently, I have quite a thing about textures. It was Alison who noticed it during the course of multiple conversations while we were away. I can't walk around in my bare feet as even a crumb underfoot upsets me. Ice cream is not meant to have bits in it. Minestrone soup just shouldn't exist (with all those lumpy bits and slimy pasta in it). I don't eat any kind of fat on meat, and if I find a tiny fishbone in my mouth, it's game over. I don't like milkshakes because they feel like fur on my tongue and I don't like people to shake orange squash because all the sediment mixes in and you get bits in your mouth. As for mandarin oranges, the pith and the skin on segments are a no-no. And don't talk to me about tinned peaches on the breakfast buffet. I need to pick one slice at a time to make sure no hard brown bits from the peach stone are anywhere near it as the sensation of something hard when it should be soft and juicy is awful. I could go on, but you get the idea. Of course, there's also the thong in flip-flops. The sensation of something between my toes – it's not happening. I should stop there because I could fill a whole chapter and would probably attract a diagnosis of some kind!

There were so many other things that I learned about myself on that trip. I learned that I can travel alone and enjoy my own company. I enjoy having a bedroom all to myself and not having to negotiate shower timings, breakfast, use of hangers, etc. It was my first experience of having a butler and initially that felt a bit uncomfortable, but it also meant that I didn't feel anonymous as a solo traveller. Crossing the Tasman Sea was a bit rocky and I started to feel sick, so my butler sprang into action. Every night, a travel sickness pill would be sitting on my bedside table and green apples and ginger ale would appear in my room. Alison's son had told us that the crew often used these for seasickness, so I'd asked the butler if it would be possible to provide both. 'Of course, madam, no trouble.'

On Valentine's Day, the crew started to put hearts and red roses everywhere. I didn't feel too sad, but it was the first one since Richard's death and it marked the first of several milestones that year. I wanted Alison and Derek to have time on their own to celebrate, but they insisted that I join them for dinner. They were just trying to look out for me. However, I declined. I needed some quiet time. They had a word with my butler to let him know about my circumstances, so when I called Hitesh to request room service, he said, 'It will be my pleasure, madam.' That well-mannered young Indian butler spent 20 minutes with me.

'I believe it's a difficult day for you, madam. How are you?'

We talked about a mixture of things – life, his family, his aspirations, and how I was doing. Dinner arrived under a large silver cloche and was served on a table covered with a crisp linen tablecloth. My dessert even had a fancy tuile decoration on top. I was going to be all right.

CHAPTER 14

Look – no stabilisers!

Fresh from the success of my first trip without Richard, I had a new-found sense of adventure and decided that our joint dream of travelling around the world would become my solo mission. Having felt safe on the small, five-star cruise ship, I chose to book with the same company for my first true solo adventure, with no wingmen. It was a bit like riding a bike without stabilisers for the first time. I decided on the Far East cruise that I never got to take with Richard. I'd be flying to Hong Kong for an overnight stay before boarding the ship. I decided to eat in the restaurant across the road from my hotel. Bizarrely, it was the same restaurant of 'chilli chicken' fame! Obviously, my menu choice was slightly different this time around.

Once on board ship, I decided to attend the solo travellers' meet-up for the first time. For the avoidance of any doubt, this is not a dating agency! As I walked down the corridor to orientate myself, I couldn't believe my eyes. I saw Hitesh, my butler from the previous ship, coming towards me. 'Hello, how are you, Dr Morrison?' At that moment, I knew I'd be OK. I had a similar experience later that evening when I tentatively wandered along to the solo traveller pre-dinner drinks event. My main concern about solo travelling was eating alone and feeling conspicuous, so when I turned up and found about 20 other people in similar circumstances, I relaxed. Staff were on hand to coordinate some chat and, for anyone who didn't have dinner plans, they'd make a group reservation in the restaurant of our choice.

I started talking to Nancy and Irene, two nice ladies from Canada, and felt relieved that I'd made some friends to have dinner with. Unfortunately, they'd already made reservations for the specialty restaurants for most of the subsequent evenings, as they're former work colleagues who often travel together. However, they chose to dine with the group on the first night, so we continued to chat over dinner. As we sat down at the table, a mocktail was brought over to me. No one had ordered a drink yet. I looked up, confused, but then it became clear. I caught the eye of the barman and it was Rakesh, the bartender from my New Zealand cruise. On the previous ship, I ordered a mocktail every night. As there were only two choices on the drinks menu, after two nights I'd asked Rakesh to surprise me. Every night after that, all I had to do was ask for a 'Rakesh special' and a different drink would appear. He made up different concoctions daily and named them for me according to the destination we'd visited that day. When he saw me again, a year later, he just picked up where he'd left off! I felt so cared for. Later in the cruise, I was reading my book by the pool and another mocktail arrived. There was no sign of Rakesh this time, so I went over to speak to the barman. He said, 'I share a room with Rakesh. Is my mocktail better than his?' What personalised service! I know passengers' preferences are probably logged on the system, but as the recipient of this first-class service, I felt so special.

At solo traveller drinks on the second evening, I thought I'd have to befriend new people as Nancy and Irene would be off somewhere else for dinner. However, I was overwhelmed by what happened next. They appeared for drinks and said they'd cancelled all their bookings and would like to rebook them to include me. How lovely is that? As our friendship grew, we enjoyed socialising after dinner, too. Nancy and Irene taught me how to play 'chicken feet' with a set of 12 by 12 dominoes. I loved it so much that I purchased a set when I got home and taught the family how to play. Towards the end of our trip, they also invited me to join them on holiday the following year. So, before we left the ship, we'd booked a cruise from Australia to Singapore via Bali. (Little did we know then that we'd be playing transatlantic Scrabble with each other on our phones every day for two years, and our trip to Australia would be cancelled twice due to Covid.)

This trip to the Far East took me on quite a voyage of discovery. With the exception of Hong Kong, everywhere else was new to me. In Taiwan, we visited Keelung and Kaohsiung. I booked an excursion to a hot springs bathing facility because the second half of the tour was to a geopark and its strange rock formations really interested me. However, I hadn't counted on having to wander around a huge area in my swimsuit, wearing a mandatory red bathing cap. Not a good look, is all I'm saying! I looked like a bald hippo with a burnt head. At many of the ports we were met with dancers and drummers in traditional dress, entertaining us as we left the ship. We visited a spectacular Buddhist temple complex and were taken on a tour by a female monk to see a giant golden Buddha, and later we visited dragon pagodas on a lake covered with water lilies. Our next stops took us on excursions to Manila and Coron in the Philippines. There, we took a boat trip to an island where we had to disembark into waist-deep, crystal-clear blue water, and watched a dancing display by locals in grass skirts as we ate a barbecue meal. These were the last times I'd ever be seen in a swimsuit. I hate swimsuits!

In Ho Chi Minh City, Vietnam, I watched a cultural show, ate a traditional meal, had some clothes made at a tailor's shop and went on a Mekong River cruise. The traffic in Ho Chi Minh City was interesting. No, it was terrifying! I've never seen so many motorcycles in my life and have definitely never seen so many people on a single motorbike: Mum, Dad, two children, a baby and a dog, all in flip-flops and without helmets, perched precariously on a small scooter. To cross the road you have to launch yourself into six-deep traffic and the vehicles drive around you. Quite a system! At the side of the road, I saw someone squat down and go to the toilet on the pavement. Bizarre! The Mekong River tour felt more authentic than the city centre shopping area. We sailed past longboats laden with fruit and vegetables steered by a person in a coolie hat, buildings on stilts, large tropical fruits hanging from trees, exotic flowers in the gardens and fried fish in the buffet, with heads, eyes, scales and everything cooked to be eaten. We also visited the lacquer factory, where they made pictures using crushed eggshells, as well as the local museum and a temple, thick with the smell of incense.

In Sihanoukville, Cambodia, we witnessed some distressing poverty but got a sense of ordinary life with a visit to a vibrant fruit and fish market and a school full of cute children. Mud-caked tuk-tuks ferried people around the city and we visited a local home where chickens ran free and fresh fish hung from a pole. The pavements were drowning in discarded plastic bottles outside makeshift shops with rusty tin roofs and open stalls. The contrast between the gold-plated temples and flashy casino buildings and this kind of poverty somehow felt wrong. The cruise line paid the locals to give us a taste of the real Cambodia, which provided them with much-needed income, but it felt voyeuristic and a bit unsavoury. At the temple, we were told not to give money to the beggars, who were bilateral amputees. They'd lost limbs to landmines during the war and were shuffling around on their bottoms holding up young children to beg for money. Cute children are kept off school to earn money from tourists, but the way out of poverty is education, and this encourages truancy. It was suggested that we should donate pencils to the school instead. The amputees are victims of exploded landmines laid down during the civil war between the Khmer Rouge, the government of Cambodia and other factions. Several areas have yet to be cleared of mines.

I'd booked into a five-star resort in Bangkok, Thailand, for a few days before flying home, but felt the need to book excursions because I didn't feel confident wandering around a strange city on my own. Nancy and Irene were staying on too, but had been there before and were planning on doing some shopping, their favourite pastime. I approached the concierge to ask if I could book something involving elephants. The excursions to an elephant sanctuary were too far away as I needed to be back in time for a dinner cruise with Irene and Nancy to round off our trip together. The hotel said they'd arrange a tour for me the following day. But first I had an afternoon and evening to fill. I was keen to visit the floating markets, Grand Palace and temples (Wat Pho and Wat Arun). Fortuitously, I met a couple who'd been on the same cruise and they asked if I wanted to join them for a boat trip to visit all the temples and Grand Palace and then go for an authentic Thai meal. Perfect.

The next morning, I was up early and down for breakfast before my tour. They took my temperature at the entrance to the restaurant and everyone was wearing masks, which seemed odd. Was this just what they do here? The tour guide came to reception to collect me. There was no tour bus or any other passengers. I had a private tour guide and driver all to myself for the day. We took a boat ride through the floating markets before going to a place where I must confess I did two things I'm not particularly proud of: I rode an elephant and cuddled a baby orangutan. These activities raised money to care for orphaned animals but I still feel the animals were being exploited, and for that I feel guilty. I love elephants and am obsessed with orangutans, so this adventure was hard to resist. We made it back in time for the farewell dinner cruise with my new Canadian buddies and ate a lovely feast as we cruised past the temples, illuminated beautifully against the dark sky with the reflections shimmering on the water. This trip was filled with so many special memories, but the main learning for me was that I could travel solo, make friends and enjoy exploring new pastures. Where to next?

CHAPTER 15

Washy washy

One of the potential problems on a ship is the outbreak of diseases such as norovirus, which causes sickness and diarrhoea. Hand hygiene is the best protection, particularly where the ship buffet is concerned. This is true for hospital wards, too. When I was working, sometimes whole wards would be shut down because of it. Occasionally, I've witnessed a ship's health and safety measures ramp up, with buffets suddenly being closed and staff wearing gloves to serve food. However, there's always someone on duty at the restaurant entrance with hand sanitiser, saying 'washy washy' or similar to remind you to use the hand sanitiser provided.

Halfway through the Far East cruise, we'd started to hear reports of an infection in China which was causing some concern worldwide. The self-service buffet closed, staff started wearing gloves and masks and it was noticeable that the furniture on the ship, handles and balconies were all being washed down regularly, which I'd never noticed before. By the time we disembarked in Thailand, it was clear that we were being chased down the coast by this new infection. That was why the staff were all wearing masks and taking our temperatures before we entered the dining room. It all felt a bit surreal. I must admit, I don't watch TV on holiday, so I was pretty clueless as to what was going on. On the way home, the man next to me coughed all the way through the flight. Some other new cruise friends, who were sitting directly behind me, tapped my shoulder, mouthing, 'What the f***?!' The man didn't speak to me until we landed, when he removed his headphones. I said to him, 'Have you been on holiday?' His reply was, 'Yes, I went to China, but there was some infection going on there, so I travelled to Thailand.' My new friends emailed me a week later to make sure I got home OK and to ask if I'd caught the 'Chinese virus' from the coughing man on the aeroplane. Fortunately, I was symptom free, but little did I know that this was the start of my Covid journey.

Despite that experience, I had to go into lockdown two weeks before the rest of the UK. We were calling it coronavirus by that point. I had a phone call from my friend Marion to say that she'd recently returned from a ski holiday and had developed a head cold. She'd been contacted by the public health department at the hospital to say that someone on her flight had tested positive for this new virus from China. Anyone who'd been in contact and had flu-like symptoms needed to be tested. She tested positive and it was mandatory at that stage for new cases to be hospitalised. The government and NHS didn't know what they were dealing with. She was one of the first five cases in Scotland. We'd met for coffee and a chat for several hours a few days before she became symptomatic. All of her contacts had to be monitored on a daily basis and were told to self-isolate for two weeks.

In Scotland, we went into full lockdown on 23 March 2020. I remember it well, as it was my birthday, the anniversary of Richard's death, and Fraser temporarily left home the same day. We had no idea what the world was about to embark upon. What a strange time. It was a bit like a bereavement. I'd lost Richard exactly two years before, but now I'd actually be living on my own for the first time and have no meaningful social contact for a protracted period. It was quite an introduction to an empty nest. When couples experience this phenomenon, they may find it difficult adjusting to the change in parental relationship and roles, plus a sense of loss, fear or grief when their last child moves out. I'd already done some adjusting to being widowed but the lack of any other human being living in the house definitely felt like another loss. Looking back at that period is quite difficult for me. There are few anchors or events in my memory to latch onto. It's as if pieces of a jigsaw are all mixed up in my head and lots of them are blank.

When you find yourself stranded on a desert island (not that I have personal experience of that – not yet anyway), it helps to be able to communicate with others. One worldwide communication system recognised by everyone is Morse code, which is a series of dots and dashes. It's odd, but when I found myself stranded alone on my own home 'island' during lockdown, I started using pointillism as a coping strategy. One dot at a time, I'd create detailed pen and ink artwork. Just in case you ever need it, SOS is the most common distress signal in Morse code, and it's just three dots, three dashes and three dots. Millions of us would experience distress as our isolation and loneliness grew. The positive for me was that I had time to perfect my pointillism technique. However, I needed thousands and thousands of dots for that, but no dashes.

I recall the daily mixed messages from the government about how many people had died; how many, if any, people we could socialise with, and for how long; and how far we could travel from our home. Guidance fluctuated and didn't always make a lot of sense. The one consistent message was to WASH YOUR HANDS! I'd been practising that on the cruise ship. I'm not a rule breaker by nature, so I tended to follow the guidance as best I could. I made a face mask from a grey sports bra before you could buy masks. I wore it once to the supermarket, which was quite surreal. I exercised daily, walking around our

95

estate or the golf course where my house is situated. I visited my 90-year-old mum for a chat on her doorstep, to drop off her shopping, as I was in her bubble as a main carer. I'd soon become a hairdresser (for Mum and my own fringe). I entered the supermarket when the traffic light at the door said I was allowed to go in and bought a few extra toilet rolls (as did the rest of the population, just in case they ran out).

I also learned how to use Zoom for communication via the internet. I took part in weekly Zoom meetings for BNI and Rotary and participated in quizzes and other activities. Despite the regular use of Zoom, I lost count of how many times I had to say, 'Your mic's not switched on. You'll need to turn on your camera; we can't see you.' We stood on the doorstep and clapped for the NHS and other essential workers every evening at a set time. It definitely brought a sense of community, seeing neighbours and waving across the street to them. It was nice to see whole families out walking their dogs or riding their bikes together. How lucky I was to live in a semi-rural area. How did people cope with children in a high-rise flat, with no garden, trying to deliver home schooling and continuing to work from home, sitting on their bed with a laptop on the dressing table?

Initially, I delivered Mum's shopping to her back door while wearing my mask, and I'd stand and talk to her just to ensure she had some social contact. When regulations eased a little and we'd started to get vaccinated, I made the decision to be fully in a bubble with Mum, so I could enter her home for a proper visit while still wearing my mask and washing my hands. As time dragged on I began to think, 'What if something happens to Mum, like a stroke or a heart attack, and she dies?' Her last few months will have been miserable and isolated, trying to avoid Covid. We knew there was a slightly increased risk if I went into her home, but her mental health was much better as a result of my decision. She didn't catch Covid until she went into hospital after falling down some stairs and fracturing her femur. Miraculously, at age 91, she survived with minimal symptoms. The staff were clearly struggling, but one standout memory from that time was a member of the nursing staff crocheting a small blanket for Mum's knee and staff suggesting that she order a baked potato. Then they brought in a prawn cocktail as a treat. These small acts of kindness restored my faith in humanity.

I had to attend a small funeral in Aberdeen for Richard's cousin's husband, wearing a mask and sitting apart from everyone else. We were lucky to be able to say our goodbyes to Jim. During lockdown there were thousands who were denied being with loved ones for their last moments in hospital, being present for the birth of babies, having contact with relatives in care homes or attending the funerals of loved ones.

Working from home and having less ability to socialise actually had a positive impact on Fraser as it allowed him time to study remotely to complete his university degree while still working full time. Sadly, Jill had to work throughout the pandemic as she's in the prison service. The changing guidelines and restrictions meant her job role was unclear, which triggered a relapse of her obsessive-compulsive disorder and her first-ever OCD-linked sickness absence. However, something positive resulted from her experience. Her self-advocacy improved and she's now much more assertive. I feel sorry for the young people who started work during this time. Working from home meant reduced opportunities to have peer support and the learning by osmosis that occurs in a shared workplace or team.

Reflections on filling the retirement void

I don't think I realised until recently just how much my sense of self was tied up with my job title. Giving up something that defines you can be quite daunting. I had no experience as a retiree or widow, and no formal training as an artist or writer. Going on to call myself an 'artist' and later 'author' out loud and on social media helped cement this change for me, even if I didn't believe I could call myself those things in the beginning!

Interestingly, other people started to believe it before me. Receiving positive feedback about my work gradually allowed me to challenge my self-doubt and my self-belief blossomed. It's fascinating how our identity can be so linked to a title. I used to tell patients that their illness or offence didn't define them as a person, although for years I let my job title define me, and it felt odd to leave it behind.

Filling the retirement void has been a bit like trying to find and fit pieces of a jigsaw puzzle together without having the box lid with the picture on the front. So, the picture, destination or retirement plan was unclear. That might have felt daunting until I realised that I could create whatever picture I wanted. I guess when I get stuck with a real jigsaw, I start looking for pieces with certain physical characteristics that may fit the space. Finding activities that fitted my desired characteristics or preferences was really quite similar. Just like a jigsaw piece, it may look as if it will fit, but it doesn't and you have to try again. I guess that's how I viewed the things I tried, and let's face it, I tried a few. Reframing the absence of a picture on my retirement jigsaw box as an opportunity to be in charge of my own destiny was fundamental to what happened next.

Retirement can prove to be quite a learning curve, but the good news is that it affords you the opportunity to try new things and experiment, without significant commitment or risk, until you discover what fulfils you. The trick is to learn how to feel comfortable in your own space. I was recently discussing this with my retired psychiatrist friend Diane, who lost her husband when her children were very small. She also emerged from bereavement determined to seize the day while she still has her health. Independently, we've developed similar mindsets and have both experienced fulfilling but very different retirements. When I think back to the death of my other friend Diane, from BNI, it reinforces the importance of living life to the fullest every day as none of us knows what tomorrow will bring.

Here are some of the guidelines I set for myself, which might work for you too:

★ If you get an offer to socialise, allow yourself to say yes.
★ Try to fill the week. There are no wrong moves, so don't overthink things. Each experience takes you a step closer to understanding what you need to fulfil you in retirement, even if all you do is clarify that the current activity isn't part of the fulfilment plan! Suspend judgement.
★ Give yourself permission to try completely new things. Avoid rejecting ideas without trying them because you might just surprise yourself. You don't know what you might be missing. If it doesn't bring you happiness, drop it!
★ Every day is a gift, so live life to the max. This will look different for everyone, be it learning a new language, pottering in the garden or going on an expedition to Antarctica. More of that later!
★ Surround yourself with positive people and fulfilling activities. Avoid 'mood hoovers'. If you feel the energy draining from you mid-conversation as you're faced with a wave of negativity, remember you get to choose who you spend time with in future.
★ Don't put off until tomorrow the things you can do today. Don't have regrets; you can't go back.
★ Avoid future 'if only' and 'what if' conversations. Less planning, more doing.
★ Accept support when offered – a problem shared and all that. Navigating change doesn't have to be a solo pursuit.
★ Don't allow assumptions or concerns about what other people think or expect from you to limit your ideas or options. Identify what matters to you and pursue that.
★ Be good to yourself and focus on your health and wellbeing.
★ Take lots of photographs. You can't go back and take them. They become cherished memories later in life, especially when someone close dies.

Focusing too much on creating a detailed plan for your retirement can prevent you from reacting to what's happening around you. My advice is, don't be afraid to deviate from the plan. You're in charge of your own script. Refuse to let fear of failure stop you from heading down a new path. The important thing is to remain open to new opportunities.

PART 3

All aboard the author coaster

CHAPTER 16

Write that book

In the summer of 2021, everyone was struggling with the Covid restrictions. I'd continued to work on my memoir as there was no shortage of free time to do it. Life really had moved online as a way of retaining some semblance of social contact. People were pivoting their businesses to try to earn money in new ways as their traditional income streams had dried up. Award-winning author and motivational speaker Michael Heppell was impacted like everyone else. There were no large venues booking speakers; everything had closed down. Michael decided to start Write That Book, an online course designed to motivate people who were contemplating writing a book to get it done. I'd written most of mine by this point but wasn't sure how to take it to the next level and get it published. It was a combination of factors: lack of knowledge, imposter syndrome and fear of failure. I researched how to find an agent and publisher and it all seemed a bit daunting, but I believed that was the proper way to do it, so I started targeting agents who specialise in memoirs. It's a less popular genre, so that limited my options. Unhelpfully, they all asked for different things, but typically they wanted the first three chapters or a set number of words. This was frustrating for me, as the first three chapters of my memoir didn't contain any of the work-related stories that might give them more of a flavour of what it was about. Daunted but undeterred, I sent some off with a covering letter. Most of the agents' websites said that, if they were interested, they'd get back to me within three months. It was like sending my work into the abyss. I'd been told I only needed one 'yes' and that lots of authors get rejected, but that's no consolation when you're scanning emails and mail every day to no avail. Very few send a 'not for us, thanks' response, but at least I knew where I stood if they did, however disappointing it might have been. Fortunately, two agents did respond positively, saying the content was interesting, and I even had a Zoom call with one to explore the idea further. They didn't think it was quite there yet and suggested further work on the manuscript.

It was around this time that I saw the Facebook ad for Michael's Write That Book course. Initially it was a free, one-week intensive offering, with Zoom chats and challenges. You submitted your work in the Facebook group for peer feedback. People developed draft titles, front cover designs, blurbs for the back cover, did quick sprints of writing and so on. It was pretty full on. In terms of having a sense of community, positive reinforcement and motivation to keep going, it ticked a lot of boxes. Not surprisingly, it ended with the offer of a paid Write That Book masterclass over several months, with Zoom group teaching and chats, a Facebook group, individual coaching, accountability groups, intensive online accelerator weekend events and access to a library of pre-recorded interviews with industry experts such as publishers and social media and marketing experts.

Everyone took something different from the course. For me, the increased focus and motivation to get my book over the line was the main thing. Having written most of the content already, I was interested to hear about the experiences of others in the group who'd tried different routes to publication. There was a big push towards self-publishing on the course, but for me, this wasn't an option. I wanted the book to be of good quality and not damage my professional reputation. I needed help in navigating confidentiality issues too, as this was a medical memoir and I needed editorial support to make sure that my storytelling was well written with a strong voice.

I watched two videos that helped immensely. One was by Sue Richardson, publishing director of The Right Book Company, a business book publisher. She generously offered a free 30-minute discovery call for all course participants who were looking for advice, even if their work wasn't in her genre. I took Sue up on her offer. Our call lasted over an hour and was quite enlightening. She talked about business books not necessarily selling in high volumes. The authors often use their books to enhance their credibility and build their business in their chosen field. Our chat took an interesting turn when Sue asked me why I was writing the book.

'Is it a legacy piece or a mission?'

I told her that, initially, it was a legacy for my children, but then I thought that if I could publish it professionally, perhaps I could sell it and influence the thinking of a wider audience around the destigmatisation of mental illness. Then she asked if there was anything else I'd want it to do. My response was not pre-planned at all. I tend to think aloud, so I sometimes surprise myself with what comes out of my mouth! Almost jokingly, I said, 'If I could become a cruise line speaker and talk about the stories in my book, I'd get to go on cruises, which I love, and hit an international audience. Win–win!'

To my surprise, she told me that this would make it a business book, because I'd be using it to enhance my profes-sional credibility and increase the chances of being booked as a speaker. She said that memoir wasn't their normal genre, but she'd be willing to work with me on that basis. Wow, what a turnaround! In that moment, my off-the-cuff daydream became a full-blown aspiration and goal. Let's do this! It was a truly pivotal moment.

The hybrid route to publishing involves quite a significant financial investment, but I was fortunate in that, having just retired, I had the money to invest in myself to achieve my dream. There was no expectation that I'd ever recoup the money, but I firmly believed I could develop a good quality product. As I said, self-publishing wasn't an option for me, especially as it required me to do more than just write the damn thing. During the course, I'd learned that if you find an agent (and that's hard), they'll try to sell the book to a publisher. If a big publisher buys it, they pay the author an advance and the publisher owns the book. They can publish, or not, when they want to (apparently there's often at least a two-year delay due to publishing schedules), and they can change the name of the book and alter the content. I didn't want anyone changing the name or content, especially as it's a memoir, with confidentiality to consider, and the title means a lot to me. You don't receive great royalties either as they recoup your advance from the profit they make from sales. What they do have is access to the shelves of big bookshops such as Waterstones, which is unlikely if you're self-published. With The Right Book Company, I'd have much more control and influence over what mattered to me and also get higher royalties. I'd also still have access to all the specialists that would be available at a big publishing house, for example a developmental editor, copy editor, proofreader, typesetting, graphic design and foreign rights, with some marketing and promotion advice thrown in for good measure. I'd be dealing with a small group of accessible professionals rather than entering a huge, impersonal machine. So, I signed the contract and we were off on our journey.

I employed Lauren, the virtual assistant from my business group, to type the first draft. At a later stage, I had some additional support from my old PA Karen and eventually mastered making changes and communicating via Google

Docs while I was working with Bev, my superb developmental editor. For a technophobe, this was a huge achievement. It was heartening to discover that my writing style was quite good. Bev edited all the text but didn't fundamentally change the content or writing style. I'd asked her for assistance with ordering the content in a logical manner. I'd initially tried making the content chronological and then splitting it up into themes as an alternative format. Bev explained that part of her role was to take all the anecdotes and string them together like pearls on a necklace. I like that analogy. In order to keep to the agreed word count and ensure the content was relevant, we'd need to cull some of the material. When it's your own personal story and you're emotionally invested in all of it, this is a difficult task. Bev was so helpful with this. She asked me to clarify the message I wanted to get across and then challenged me to ask how each particular anecdote enhanced the message. If it didn't, it was out. It felt a bit brutal but necessary and I absolutely couldn't have achieved that by myself.

Not all the anecdotes are funny, bizarre or scary stories that contribute to the message about the destigmatisation of mental illness. I needed to include contextual anecdotes about my own history, which influenced my core values, drivers and morals, and the doctor I became. I learned a lot about myself in the process. It matters to me that people with a mental illness are seen first as human beings and aren't defined by their illness or, in the case of mentally disordered offenders, by their offence. Being non-judgemental when people have committed an illness-related offence is crucial if you want to treat and rehabilitate them.

It's almost impossible to work with offenders if you're judgemental. You may need to treat someone who's raped a child or murdered a pensioner. You need to be able to see the person, while identifying and managing any illness or offending-related risks. My strength was in establishing a trusting relationship with patients, taking a detailed history from them and producing a person-centred holistic care plan and risk-management plan. I preferred an open and honest style of communication and took time to prioritise explaining the rationale for a decision or boundary, so that patients were invested and involved in the planning of their care, even if they didn't always agree with it. The challenge, then, was to capture this message within the memoir.

Chapter 17

I don't talk to dead bodies...

After three months, Bev and I felt the manuscript was ready to hand over. Bev asked me for my thoughts about the book title and cover design. *I Don't Talk to Dead Bodies* was pretty fixed in my mind as the title, as I always used it to explain what a forensic psychiatrist was, and what it wasn't, at the start of lectures. A forensic psychiatrist deals with the interface between the criminal justice system and psychiatry, ie mentally disordered offenders. Typically, a forensic psychiatrist will provide expert opinion for the courts in serious murder and rape cases, run prison psychiatric clinics, work in a locked psychiatric facility with mentally disordered offenders or manage mentally disordered offenders in the community. I did all of the above at one point or another during my 32 years within the NHS. At no point did I talk to dead bodies! I wanted the subtitle to mention forensic psychiatry and imply that this was a fun read and not a serious, in-depth academic text or exposé of case studies about mentally disordered serial killers. As I've mentioned, we eventually agreed on *I Don't Talk to Dead Bodies: The curious encounters of a forensic psychiatrist.*

I got to work on ideas for the front cover and only presented one idea to marketing director Paul, who guided me through the production process. I wanted to use a cartoon image as I believed it would show that this was a light-hearted, non-academic look at a serious subject. I wanted to portray a psychiatrist's couch in the image as that immediately orientates a potential reader to the subject matter, although in reality most forensic psychiatrists neither have nor use a couch. I'd be talking about the criminal mind, so an image of the brain with handcuffs came to mind. I decided to make the brain the patient, so gave it arms and legs and tackety boots. There's a chapter in the book called 'Mr Onion Man', which talks about a communication aid I used with children, which involved dismantling my stethoscope and drawing a little onion man with tackety boots inside the flat section that sits against your chest wall. I'd tell the patient that I'd brought Mr Onion Man to help me examine them, as a distraction, and then let them have a go at listening to their own heart. Mr Brain, the cartoon criminal mind of a mentally disordered offender, was a homage to Mr Onion Man. I drew the picture using the pen and ink pointillism technique I'd developed during lockdown. It was my one and only draft. When I showed it to Paul, he loved it. And so, the cover design was nearly nailed. Trying to choose a background colour and font combo was so difficult. Eventually, the designer sent several options and I let the kids decide. They chose well.

The production process was clearly timetabled over a six-month period. I had no idea what copy editors, typesetters and proofreaders did, but I trusted the process. At one point I got a message from Andrew, the production manager, saying that there were very few changes required but could he suggest a change from 'Glasgow' to 'Scotland' in one particular story, where I discussed deep-fried Mars Bars having been invented in Glasgow? He'd researched this and they were actually invented in Stonehaven. Who knew that this level of background checking goes into publishing a quality text? I was impressed. He also confessed that my book was the first one he'd copy edited that had made him cry. I didn't set out to make people cry, but felt proud that I'd told my story in a sufficiently honest and unfiltered way to elicit such emotion in the reader. When we'd worked together on the book, Bev had suggested that the last two chapters should remain untouched. They were written just after Richard died and were powerful, emotional accounts of a difficult time. Since the book has been published, many people have reported laughing out loud while reading the book and then sobbing uncontrollably at the end.

Paul asked if I could think of anyone who could write an endorsement, and I eventually came up with three names. Thankfully, they all agreed, for different reasons. The main endorsement was from Leslie Riddoch, an award-winning Scottish journalist, broadcaster and author. She also happens to be the sister of one of my friends from my university badminton days. She was his 'best man', in a peach dress, so it was a bit of a personal angle to add to my email request. She generously agreed to read my book and, if she liked it, write an endorsement. And she did. Her endorsement was glowing. It clearly demonstrated that she'd read the book and some of the themes resonated with her.

My next endorsement was from Michael Heppell, who'd facilitated the Write That Book course that had helped me to get my book over the line and introduced me to my publisher. Another endorsement was from Charlie Lawson, who's probably less well known, but is also a published Right Book Company author. I'd met Charlie via BNI, as at the time he was BNI's national director in the UK. He'd presented me with my '100' award, which was quite a big deal, as it's difficult to achieve and it was really nice that he presented it to me. I believed he had some influence across the BNI network and thought his endorsement might be helpful in that respect. In the process, he also commissioned a painting of his partner's cat!

During the Write That Book masterclass journey, we were strongly encouraged to develop a Facebook page, a year in advance of a publication if possible, in order to grow a tribe of followers who'd hopefully become invested in the book and want to pre-order one. This wasn't straightforward for a technophobe like me, but it was more than just the lack of technical ability that held me back. A Rhona Morrison Author page was required, as I already had a Rhona Morrison Art page. But I wasn't a published author at that stage – I was just in the middle of writing it! How could I use that title? 'Just do it,' was the advice. 'Write about your plans, the developmental stage you're at, share snippets, get them involved in giving opinions, share potential titles and cover designs, give updates, timescales for pre-order and launch events.' So I developed a Rhona Morrison Author page and decided to post twice a week. The advice from social media experts was to post more frequently, scheduling several posts to come out over a period of time, but I don't like being bombarded with profile-raising posts that have limited value in terms of content, so I wasn't about to do that. I had to develop a new internal radar system to search for content to include. It got easier over time. I added my book blurb to my website too, which previously had only been for my art business. It meant that people could pre-order a signed copy of my book directly from me. Financially this was the best option for me, as I'd have 500 paperback copies of my book as part of my publishing contract. With more than 200 pre-orders on my website, I had the logistical challenge of posting out 200 parcels in one day, pre-launch. I split the task between two local Post Offices and sweet-talked the postmistresses with the offer of a free signed copy as a thank you. Fortunately, they both agreed to help. It was great to have this initial sales boost, but I hadn't factored in that these sales wouldn't show on Amazon and therefore wouldn't count towards my sales ranking in my genre's bestseller list. Most of these people wouldn't think to post a review on Amazon either, as they hadn't bought it there. However, all was not lost, as my Rhona Morrison Author page appeared to have reached a wider audience and I saw that I had pre-sales on Amazon, too.

I asked my BNI colleagues if anyone knew a freelance journalist who might write an article for me pre-launch, as an extra promotional activity. Yet again, my colleagues came to the rescue. I shared an electronic draft of my book with the journalist and he kindly agreed to produce an article, which he subsequently sold to the *Scottish Mail on Sunday*. I saw the article and although it was clearly written to sell newspapers, it did try to cover the message within the book and didn't identify any patients. However, I do mention some details about a particular case in my book as it had already been covered in the national press at the time of the offence and court case, so it was already in the public domain. I used it to highlight the message that sometimes mental illness makes good people do bad things, and it was my job to find them, treat them and rehabilitate them, not judge them. It was also used to highlight the human being behind the sensational headlines. However, no names or photographs were used as I didn't want to sensationalise the case myself.

The paper sent a photographer to do a photoshoot at my home and they eventually published a two-page colour spread. To my horror, the editor had decided to look back through their archives and dig out the article about the story I'd referred to, including the patient's photo and name, which was the complete opposite of my intention. I was mortified and it caused me many sleepless nights. However, I can't deny the fact that the article and publicity helped to sell books. The day after the article was published, BBC Radio Scotland got in touch, inviting me to do a live interview about my book on their Thursday morning show. As a result, I now seem to be on the BBC's list of experts and have been invited onto a few radio show panels. I've even advised a researcher for a TV production. By that Friday, I was number one on the Amazon new-release chart for my genre and the book wasn't even out yet. (The book went on to be in the top 100 for my genre fairly consistently for two years after publication.)

CHAPTER 18

Talk to me

When Covid restrictions had eased, my solo traveller friends Nancy and Irene from Toronto planned a trip to a castle in Scotland for a friend's rescheduled birthday party. Their friendship group fascinated me, as they travelled all over the world for big birthday celebrations, including South Africa, Scotland and Europe. They invited me to meet them for a lovely lunch before they returned home. The day after our meeting, Irene called to say that she'd tested positive for Covid at the airport and was having to self-isolate in Edinburgh. A couple of days later, Nancy contacted me to say she'd tested positive on returning to Canada. Shortly after that, I developed a sore throat, a husky voice and two lines on my Covid test. The timing couldn't have been worse, as I'd booked Ian Housley from Dormdust recording studio in England to record my audiobook for four days the following week. I had to cancel travel, hotel and studio arrangements and reschedule everything for a few weeks later when I had my voice back and a negative test result.

Ian, his wife, and their little dog Oban made me feel so welcome. We've kept in touch since. In fact, they've invited me to come and stay at their house when I record audiobook number two. It felt a bit weird being in a recording studio, surrounded by guitars and microphones, with 'egg box' soundproofing on the wall, looking through the glass panel at Ian with all his sound equipment. I had to read from an electronic copy of my book on an iPad so that you couldn't hear any turning of pages. It was an interesting project for Ian too, and for the first time he said he felt emotionally invested in the subject matter as I read it.

Ian said that he'd recommend people who like to read paperbacks or ebooks to at least listen to the last two chapters of my first audiobook because they're so powerful and personal. I told someone this recently and, after listening to my audiobook, all six and a half hours of it, she agreed with him. What started as an audiobook project to make sure that Mum, who's partially sighted, could read my book, has turned into a very popular form of my memoir, now outselling the other formats on Amazon. I still sell a lot of paperbacks at Meet the Author events in libraries and colleges, as people are always keen to get a signed copy. However, it does seem that audiobooks are now very popular. It just shows how trends move over time with people using technology to listen to books on their way to work on the train, in the car and when out walking their dogs. I've only recently tried audiobooks in the car and I must confess that I'm quite enjoying them.

Having completed the audiobook recording, I realised I'd been signed by the publisher on the basis that I aspired to become a cruise line speaker. So, I thought I'd better start to hone my speaking skills in advance of my book being published. I decided to join the Professional Speaking Association (PSA) for the Scotland region as a way of meeting fellow speakers and developing my practical skills and stagecraft. We meet monthly and have a series of established speakers who share gems of knowledge and practical skills with us. In addition, there's the opportunity to give a short presentation, to showcase new material and get constructive feedback.

When I joined, they told me about Speaker Factor, a UK-wide competition that takes place every year. Regional heats are held in advance of the UK final at the annual PSA summit. I was persuaded to enter, but the heats were taking place on the day I was flying back from the Rotary International Convention in Houston, Texas. I was overwhelmed by the huge number of like-minded Rotarians from every corner of the globe and the inspiring charitable work being carried out. We'd fitted in some touristy activities too, including riding Segways around the city centre, attending a baseball match and visiting NASA. After the conference, I'd managed to sneak in almost an extra week, staying with my cruise buddies Texan quizzers Karen and Jimmy before flying home. Initially, I'd contacted them to see if we could meet up for lunch while I was in Houston, but they were a three-and-a-half-hour drive away and invited me to come and stay for a few days instead. I had to take an internal flight. We'd started as acquaintances in New Zealand and, by the end of my rather cheeky visit to their home in Longview, my generous hosts ended up as firm friends.

Despite the timing challenges and potential jetlag, I'd decided to enter the Speaker Factor competition and had practised my ten-minute presentation multiple times, including on the plane (in my head, obviously – premium economy doesn't include a lecture from me!). You're disqualified if you run over, so timing is everything. Sadly, there were significant delays at Heathrow and after all the practice and angst leading up to it, I never got to compete. I'd have to wait another 12 months.

As the new date approached, I practised my talk, which was a tiny snippet from one of the anecdotes in my memoir. I told the story of my retirement cupcakes and how they linked to the story about a psychotic sex offender dropping his trousers and masturbating in my office while I was trying to take his sexual history. I decided that props would be helpful as no PowerPoint slides were allowed. I made a replica of one of the cupcakes, which made specific reference to this incident, decorating it with male genitals made out of marzipan, and sprayed them with edible gold food spray, just to show I'd made an effort! It was nerve-racking presenting to a room full of professional speakers, knowing I was being judged and would get feedback immediately afterwards.

There were several entrants that night. Unfortunately for me, a new member of the group called Kevin Quantum was also taking part. He's an experienced stage performer and delivers his magic show all over the world. He regularly sells out shows at the 700-seat Assembly Rooms at the Edinburgh Fringe. During his engaging and polished talk, he also managed to fit in a great magic trick. The audience were impressed. Follow that! He was amazing and I knew he would make a superb candidate to represent Scotland. He's also very humble, too. I was agonisingly near and yet so far from getting through. Just before the competition began at the Glasgow venue, Kevin had contacted the president to say that he'd injured his Achilles tendon that morning, was now wearing a huge boot to immobilise his ankle and couldn't drive. Right up until a few minutes before we were about to start the competition, we thought he wasn't going to make it, and I was thinking that maybe, just maybe, I'd have a chance of winning. Then he hobbled in and went on to take the crown. You're only able to enter once, so I'd picked the wrong year to enter. Damn you, Heathrow Airport!

CHAPTER 19

Beyoncé, Bieber... and me

When it came to arranging my book launch, I wasn't too sure how big a deal to make of it. Matters were taken out of my hands when Fraser's friend Adam announced, 'I'll be doing your book launch.' I didn't know what to expect because, as far as I knew, he loved performing in musical theatre shows and was a trainee primary school teacher. However, little did I know he also has his own very successful company. He's a global social media consultant, brand activation specialist, host and presenter, who's been involved with the ITV series *Dancing on Ice* and national awards ceremonies, and also manages social influencers. He took me under his wing, discussed my vision and we viewed some venues. I'd be having a press launch in the afternoon and a big launch event in the evening, in the 100-seater studio at the Lantern House Theatre in Cumbernauld.

My editor, Bev, was able to fly up for the press launch but would have to head south again before the evening event. It was the first time we'd met in person. Adam kindly arranged for the Meat Joint restaurant in the centre of Glasgow to host the press launch. Invitations were sent to journalists, TV and radio people, actors and social influencers. Adam told me that if there wasn't a big media story that day, we'd get coverage on the BBC and STV (Scotland's ITV channel). Sadly, a drag queen who'd appeared on the popular TV show *RuPaul's Drag Race UK* died that day, so we lost some of the journalists. However, we still had entertainment journalist Bev Lyons, a presenter from Radio Clyde, an actor from the TV show *Mrs Brown's Boys* and multiple social influencers. All I had to do was turn up with a pile of free books for the attendees; Adam organised everything else. He said, 'Don't worry if the influencers only stay for ten minutes and just take a selfie with you and the book. We just need them to post about it and recommend it to their network.' In the end, they all stayed for the whole event and even participated in the Q&A session. They seemed really engaged with the subject matter. Bev interviewed me and, as planned, we shared some interview questions with the other Bev (Lyons), who'd kindly agreed to host the evening event.

I'd advertised the evening launch on my social media page and was overwhelmed by the response from my network, far and wide. Among the 100-strong audience of smiling faces were family, friends, Rotarians, old school friends, psychiatrists, NHS colleagues, neighbours, tennis players, mahjong pals, fellow authors, BNI colleagues, university friends and more. I wasn't allowed to greet them on arrival. Adam told me, 'Once everyone is seated and Bev has done the introduction, you'll be invited onto the stage.'

So, there I was backstage, getting my headset fitted and checked. I had no idea if people would actually turn up. I'd insisted on including two short videos and a short PowerPoint presentation as part of the proceedings because I wanted to set the context and allow my editor Bev and audiobook engineer Ian Housley to have their say as they'd played such integral roles in the process. Bev Lyons entered to rapturous applause.

'Good evening, I'm Bev Lyons, otherwise known as "Showbiz Lyons". I'm more used to interviewing Beyoncé and Bieber, but tonight I'm going to be interviewing Dr Rhona Morrison.' More rapturous applause ensued. At this point, I made my entrance. We'd set up the stage to have two armchairs and a small table, for a cosy chat, with the screen behind us. We ended up talking for about an hour, which included a short reading from the book's prologue. After that there was time for a book signing and photos. Despite almost everyone already having purchased a signed copy of my book from my website, I still sold 30 books that night. It all went really well.

I'd also heard about virtual book tours via someone in my Facebook author group. This involved sending several copies to the organiser. She distributes them to her list of book reviewers who write book blogs. Over the course of the specified book tour week, they would post their review on their allotted day. There was no guarantee that they'd be positive reviews, just an agreement that an independent review would be posted on Amazon and shared with their network, on their blog or whatever social media platform they used. Fortunately, I received four- or five-star reviews from all the bloggers.

According to my publisher, 50-plus Amazon reviews is an important milestone as at that point the reach of the book becomes more significant. At the point of writing, two years post publication, I've had more than 270 reviews, with the majority being five star. I'm pleased with that. However, it's important to have a range of reviews. It proves that it's not just all your family and friends writing good reviews. With my book in particular, the subject matter may attract people looking for in-depth case histories of serial killers. If so, they'll be sorely disappointed. One person wrote in their review that they thought I used too many exclamation marks. How dare they!!! Ha ha!!! Feedback is always helpful. It makes you stop and take stock, even if you don't always agree with it.

When the book was first published, I dreaded the response in case people were offended, upset, angry, disappointed, hated my writing style, weren't interested and so on. The doubt and feelings of inadequacy were powerful. I was firmly strapped into the 'author coaster' and it was too late to get off. The emotional roller coaster was terrifying. However, when I started to get really positive, unsolicited feedback, especially from strangers, the emotions became overwhelmingly positive. Gradually, I began to feel that I could inhabit the role of author after all. I might've been saying it on Facebook but I didn't really believe it until that point. As with all things we do or say in life, not everyone is going to like them, and that's OK. Not everyone likes Harry Potter books, but J K Rowling is selling plenty of books. Not everyone likes the idea of attending a muddy music festival, but Glastonbury is still a sellout. You just need to know your target audience and try to engage with them.

Reflections on boarding the author coaster

Writing my memoir and boarding the author coaster was one of the best decisions I've ever made, but it also led to the most sleepless nights and fluctuations in self-confidence that I've ever experienced. I was entering completely uncharted territory and felt woefully unprepared for the task ahead of me. I was repeatedly reminded of how immensely powerful words can be. In the blink of an eye, a motivating word of encouragement or a negative comment could send the emotional roller coaster either trundling skyward or plummeting to the ground, taking my self-confidence with it.

I've always believed that feedback should be constructive but the author coaster experience reminded me just how damaging words can be if they're not used judiciously. When my daughter Jill read my first attempt at Chapter 1, her comments were, 'That's not you, it's all flowery!' That was powerful! I started again, this time trying to capture my authentic voice. Her honest feedback was incredibly helpful. I guess my advice here would be that, whether you're writing a book or not, you should strive to be your authentic self.

PART 4

More leaps of faith

CHAPTER 20

Antarctic explorer

Having cruised annually for nearly 20 years, by 2023 I'd travelled around Europe as well as the Baltics, the Far East, Australia, New Zealand, the US, the Arabian Gulf and China. Technically, I'd visited six out of seven continents, but there was still one missing, which was perhaps the most intriguing: Antarctica. Travelling there isn't for the faint hearted, especially if you're a solo traveller. My credit card groaned, but I knew I'd be looked after, having previously travelled to New Zealand and the Far East with the same luxury cruise line, plus I'd be on an expedition ship with only 250 passengers. Various questions swirled around my head. Will I be able to buy waterproof trousers that fit my big bum? Will the big red anorak provided as part of the trip zip up around my stomach? How many hats, fleeces, socks, buffs and gloves will I need? Will I be able to jump onto a Zodiac boat from the ship without falling in the water? How cold will it be? Will my iPhone work as a camera at these temperatures?

Shortly after I booked, I received an email from Karen, my Texan cruise buddy from the New Zealand trip, whom I'd gone on to visit in Texas, to ask if I'd booked any more cruises. When

I told her I'd just booked a trip to Antarctica, she said she'd always wanted to go, but her husband Jimmy had told her no way. Fast-forward a few days and a second email arrived. 'I've booked Antarctica. I'm coming with you. Jimmy doesn't want to come.' Fast-forward another few days and yet another email arrived. 'Jimmy says I can't go because it will be our wedding anniversary while I'm away. I just told him it's Rhona's fault; she booked it, so either he'll have to wait until I get back or come with me. So, he's coming.' That meant one had become three. At around the same time, my two Canadian cruise buddies, Nancy and Irene, got in touch and I told them about Antarctica. They're global travellers and are always trying to 'bag' new countries every year to add to their long list. Neither had been to Antarctica, and so three became five.

Everything I'd read about Drake's Passage, the body of water between Cape Horn, Chile, Argentina and the South Shetland Islands of Antarctica, was terrifying. It connects the Atlantic, Pacific and Southern Oceans and is regularly beset with storms and high seas. We'd be sailing for two days down and two days back in very choppy seas. But before that, five intrepid travellers flew into Santiago, Chile, where we spent a night in a luxury hotel and became acquainted over dinner. The next day, we flew on a small, specially chartered plane to an old military base in Puerto Williams, Chile, where we'd board the ship. The cruise line had moved to this port during the pandemic, to avoid Argentinian restrictions in Ushuaia. We were on the first flight in the morning and arrived in a snowstorm, which was quite a shock to the system following the high temperatures in Santiago, where we'd been sitting by the pool the day before. Multiple short flights were planned throughout the day to ferry all the guests to the port before our teatime departure. Unfortunately, the storm worsened, which delayed several flights. We eventually departed later than planned, in a storm. The local pilot had boarded our ship to guide us safely out of port, as per standard procedure, but when he tried to disembark onto a small boat, which was scheduled to return him to Puerto Williams, the sea was too rough and he couldn't do so safely. The captain was advised to return to port and try again in the morning. The captain, God bless him, said no, and instead took the pilot with us on an impromptu luxury cruise to the Antarctic Peninsula. You can just imagine the phone call home from the pilot. 'I won't be home in time for tea, dear. I've been kidnapped and they're taking me on a luxury cruise to Antarctica. See you in ten days.' Crew members gave him clothes and a bed and we were off on our adventure.

Shortly after we left the port, we had the mandatory safety drill. We were required to take our life jackets to a briefing at our designated muster point on deck. I was green and vomiting at the time. I had to tentatively extract myself from the toilet, where I was hanging over the sink, shuffle onto the deck and prop myself up against a pillar with a sick bag attached to my face. It wasn't my finest hour. That was the only time I've ever been sick on a cruise ship and the swell wasn't even too bad at that point. I'd taken seasickness tablets and had crystallised ginger, a green apple and some ginger ale available, on top of the acupuncture seasickness bands on my wrist, so I was trying. Fortunately, after a couple of hours I started to feel better, as I had two rocky days at sea in prospect before we hit land. I'd only be able to get to land by jumping off the side of the ship into a moving Zodiac inflatable boat, which would be bouncing through the waves, before I disembarked by swinging my legs over the edge and wading through water. This was going to be interesting.

As before, I had a butler to look after me, and he was happy to provide anything I needed. I didn't have to ask for a mocktail, as they just appeared in my room, waiting for me after each excursion. Before going on our first foray, we were required to take any clothing that we were planning to wear ashore to a checkpoint for inspection. I was so impressed by the attempts made to protect the environment from cross-contamination.

Boots and Velcro fasteners on clothing were all examined and any tiny stones or plant matter were painstakingly removed. Each time we left the ship, we were required to visit the boot room. We'd hired special, insulated knee-high rubber boots that were placed on our allocated spot on the shelf. We'd collect and return the boots to the boot room daily. Every time we returned from an excursion, we were required to go through what I like to call a human car wash. There was a mini boot wash that sprayed water while brushes rotated under the soles and around our legs to remove penguin poo and any plant matter or mud. Then we had to rinse off our boots and waterproof trousers with a handheld shower before we could remove our boots and return them to the shelf. There was always a bit of camaraderie and sharing of stories in the boot room, which was full of big, red yetis as we'd all been issued good quality polar jackets. The excursions were in allocated time slots, in small groups, to ensure that there were never more than 100 passengers on shore at any one time. This ensured that there wasn't too much disruption to the wildlife as there are strict regulations to follow in Antarctica.

An advance party of nature experts would always leave the ship first to find a safe landing point based on the tide, swell, ice and rock formation. This was out in the wild, so there were no jetties to disembark onto. The advance party would also take long poles with red flags. Once they'd established the natural route used by penguins to get to the shore, they'd use the flags to demarcate the 'penguin highway', to prevent passengers from getting in the way of the wildlife. If you stayed on the correct side of the flags, you could literally be just a few feet away from cute, waddling black-and-white penguins, but they seemed unperturbed. You may think Antarctica would be covered with ice, but it's not. In some places there were glorious vistas of snow, ice, glaciers, sculpted icebergs and crystal-clear water, but on some islands there was black volcanic sand or granite rocks.

Our expedition's lead nature expert was Neil, from Canada. What a knowledgeable and lovely human being. We came to believe that he didn't actually sleep. Every day, as well as wildlife lectures, Neil would give us a briefing. He'd summarise the plans for the following day and present the frequently changing weather maps. A vague itinerary or route had been set at the start of the cruise, but this had to be amended daily, and sometimes hourly, to try to skirt the storms and find somewhere safe and interesting to land that might also have some wildlife. Over time, we became quite adept at identifying the colours on the weather map. You can't just sail a ship wherever you want to, though, as there are other vessels in the area. They all have to negotiate and seek permission to sail in particular waters and land on a particular piece of shoreline, while not breaking the strict rules about how many people can be on shore at any one time, hence our belief that Neil stayed awake all night looking at weather maps and negotiating on our behalf. He did an excellent job. I was staggered to discover that he knew who I was. Every time we disembarked to go ashore, he would be thigh deep in water, holding onto the boat, extending a helping hand to get us off safely. He'd say, 'Right, Dr Morrison, you're next.' The restaurant staff used iPads, which no doubt had our faces, room numbers and preferences logged onto them, but not in the icy waters of Antarctica among the penguins. It was impressive!

There were many highlights, including several gentoo and chinstrap penguins parading down to the shore so they could jump off the rocks to swim and collect fish; penguin chicks nestling under their mothers; seals basking in the sun; elephant seals fighting in the distance; and giant petrel birds and snow petrel chicks nestling in the rocks. We also saw plenty of humpback whales. We initially spotted a whale blowing and the flume of water it created. As we watched, we'd sometimes be treated to seeing the fluke (the two-lobed part of the tail), a breaching whale or the joy of a mother and baby. We were there at optimal whale-spotting time as they gathered in pods to begin their migration north.

At Port Lockroy, we visited the most southerly post office in the world, where I sent postcards home and got a stamp in my passport. Not many people have that. My favourite excursion would have to be a boat trip in Paradise Bay, in all its serene, otherworldly glory. We were surrounded by bluish-white, weather-sculpted icebergs, ice floes and crystal-clear waters, with the backdrop of a huge glacier under a clear blue sky. On this trip, we'd all clambered onto the boat and, with bums precariously positioned on the side, zoomed off into open water, holding a tiny rope that ran along the outside of the inflatable. On this occasion we had the ship's wildlife video-grapher on board. Suddenly, we spotted a leopard seal basking on top of a small iceberg only feet from where we were. It was an evil-looking thing but quite unusual. 'Can we circle around the iceberg to get some shots of the leopard seal? I've never got this close before,' asked the videographer. 'Can you [meaning me] hold on to my trouser belt at the back while I lean forward to try to get some good footage? I don't want to fall in.' I obliged, firmly attaching myself as a large anchor to her bottom. We were all taking photos but it was silent apart from the odd crack in the ice or a small iceberg flipping over in the water. These were truly magical memories in the making. 'My gift to you,' said the Zodiac pilot as he turned off the engine and we floated in almost total silence in this unspoilt icy wilderness of sea, sky and ice stretching out in every direction. All we heard was the water lapping against the boat. It was picture perfect.

The images taken by the videographer would feature in the shared, take-home video of our experience in Antarctica. I was proud to play a small part in creating the leopard seal pictures. I was the anchorwoman for this show! What a privilege to experience the wonder of nature first hand. We enjoyed the experience of seeing the leopard seal and eventually it slid off the ice platform on which it had been basking and disappeared. 'I wish it would come back up,' said the videographer. I joked, 'Don't worry, I'll make its mating call and it'll reappear.' For a laugh, I started making a strange noise, and after a short while our leopard seal friend reappeared!

Back in the boot room, we met a young man from America whom Nancy and I had met in the lounge the night before. He was on his honeymoon but his wife had gone to bed early, so he had been sitting on his own. Nancy had told him about my book and the chapter called 'Tell me about your genitals', and we had had a bit of a laugh. So, here we were again, with his wife this time too. Nancy started telling him about our experience with the leopard seal and threw in the part about the seal responding to my mating call. In earshot of his new bride and other passengers, he said, 'Did you ask him to tell you about his genitals?' His wife's eyes just about popped out of her head and her jaw dropped to the floor, horrified at what her husband had just said to a stranger, obviously unaware of the conversation and banter from the night before. We left him to explain!

Having had her wedding dress hoovered to avoid taking plant material onto land, his bride did a photoshoot on the ice and then jumped into the freezing ocean in her wedding dress. After signing a medical waiver, my 75-year-old friend Jimmy took the 'polar plunge' too. Go Jimmy! He'd have bragging rights with his pals back home. A total of 70 passengers and staff took the plunge, leaping into the icy Antarctic waters with a rope attached to their waist and a small Zodiac boat and staff in the water nearby in case of emergencies. I won't wear a swimsuit or jump in feet first at the shallow end of the swimming pool, so there was no chance of me taking part!

CHAPTER 21

The benefits of abduction

My Texan friends celebrated their 50th wedding anniversary on board, so the five of us had a celebratory dinner. I'd organised a little anniversary cake from the chef and gifted them a signed copy of my book at their request. The waiters, including one called Elvis, all sang 'Congratulations'. Who knew the King would grace us with his presence on such a special day? Uh-huh, it really happened! The three of us from Canada and Scotland, who were the solo travellers in the group, went to the solo traveller meet-up most nights and met a lovely bunch of ladies from Newfoundland, New York and Belgium, so we became quite an international group. Our new friend Louise from Newfoundland had quite a story to tell. She'd been booked onto a longer Antarctic cruise, which was due to go further south, nearer to the South Pole. Unfortunately, she'd left her passport at the hotel in Santiago and was refused embarkation without it. There was no time to retrieve it before her ship set sail. The cruise line put her up in a hotel at the port and arranged for her passport to be retrieved. As it was her fault that she'd missed the ship, they could've said it was her fault and kept her money. Fortunately, they offered to let her join our ship and happy band a few days later, for a slightly shorter cruise to the Antarctic Peninsula. We benefited from her friendship... and the fact that they'd upgraded her to a large suite. She and her butler hosted a pre-dinner drinks reception for us, with champagne and canapés. Her suite was bigger than most people's flats! We've since stayed connected via Facebook and hope our paths will cross again one day.

One of the ladies was a professor. She asked not to be in any of the photos posted on Facebook as technically she was 'working from home' and this stretched that definition a little bit! She had to go off to her room to work, but there was plenty of play, too. At the end of the cruise, having navigated Drake's Passage again with a 22 ft swell, we'd be passing Cape Horn through waters that are notoriously difficult to navigate.

The following morning, there was a surprise announcement by the captain. Due to a series of chance circumstances, we'd be stopping at Cape Horn and would be able to get off and climb the cliffside steps to visit the lighthouse and huge, 24 ft-high albatross sculpture, which pays homage to the sailors who have perished attempting to round Cape Horn. The albatross is the seafaring symbol for souls lost at sea. It's estimated that more than 10,000 sailors have died there. Ships aren't allowed to navigate the waters or anchor there without a local pilot on board due to the wind, turbulent sea and rocks. But we still had our 'abducted' local pilot on board so had everything we needed to sail close and get ashore. That was just another added extra from the cruise that kept on giving. Neil was there, knee deep in water, as we disembarked the Zodiac onto slippery, wet boulders.

What did I learn from this trip? That it's lovely to travel with people you know as long as you have the flexibility to do your own thing as well. I liked setting my own timetable for the day and not having to share a room, but also having the ease of socialising with friends, whether it be for dinner, in a trivia quiz team or squeezing up against them on the edge of a Zodiac. Getting into a Zodiac from a wet metal platform on the side of a moving ship when you're dressed in a huge anorak, waterproof trousers, big rubber boots, a hat and gloves is a challenge. The ship moves up and down in the swell and the displaced water creates a wave that moves the Zodiac at a different rhythm. When one moves up, the other may move down. Stepping down six inches can suddenly become an 18-inch gap to navigate, mid-step. The ship's staff were experts in people handling and taught us how to do the firm arm grip as we held on to them while negotiating the process. The edge of the Zodiac was a huge, slippery, wet inflatable tube. You had to plonk yourself down quickly and squidge along to the side to join fellow travellers balancing on the edge, facing inwards. There were no seats or handles. On the outside of the boat there was a loose, thin rope draped around the edge, bobbing in the water. That was the only thing to hold on to, apart from the knee of the stranger next to you. I certainly grabbed a few knees to anchor myself. Once full, our guide and boat operator would take us off on yet another adventure. Disembarking on shore often involved swinging legs and bottoms over the edge of the boat into knee-deep icy water, onto slippery boulders, volcanic sandy beaches or icy landmass. Neil was always there with a strong grip. 'Welcome, Dr Morrison,' and off we trekked to meet the nature experts strategically placed to tell us about the wildlife.

On one occasion, we trekked up the side of a mountain (well, it was more like a big hill, but it was exhausting!) covered in knee-deep snow and ice, using walking poles. From a distance, we must've looked like a line of red ants climbing a huge white anthill. At the top, we could see a colony of birds. The nature expert in the orange anorak was Marcel, a professor from South America. I stopped to ask a few questions and try out my new binoculars. I was surprised by his response. 'What's all this about dead bodies?' he asked as he looked at my phone case, which was dangling in a clear plastic wallet around my neck. I'd purchased a case that features the cover of my book as a promotional exercise. It has started many conversations. I explained that it was the cover of my memoir and I was a forensic psychiatrist. 'My friend is learning English, he'd love that,' said Marcel. 'Can I take a photo of you and the phone case?' Everyone else was taking photos of the wildlife and snowy vista, but here I was, Marcel's exotic species of the day. When I landed on a different island a few days later, there he was again in his orange anorak. 'You took a photo of me last time. This time I want a selfie with you.'

It was a privilege to visit my seventh continent. There was beauty, majesty, silence, zero light pollution, and simply magical vistas and wildlife all around. I definitely kept the best until last. Nature in all its glory will forever trump any human-made treasures. The shrinking ice and endangered wildlife alert us to the fact that these wonders may disappear unless we look after them.

During our team trivia sessions each afternoon, I also managed to acquire some additional cruise buddies, newlyweds Liz and Vihan, from New York. Later in the year, they came to visit me in Scotland for a whistlestop 24 hours of castles, food and whisky tasting. It was the cruise that kept on giving. This was a once-in-a-lifetime trip. I think I may have said that about other trips, but this time I really mean it.

CHAPTER 22

Enrichment beckons...

Many people dread their 'Big 60' birthday, but 23 March 2023 was more of a big, beautiful turning point for me. I didn't think 60 was a big deal, but my family and friends had different ideas. I'd go on to be treated to beautiful gifts, including a holiday memories charm bracelet from Mum; a spa break with Jill; fancy meals; a silver jewellery-making workshop; a handmade quilt; theatre trips; an overnight stay in a castle; a bird of prey experience; alpaca trekking; a foraging lesson; a holiday to Islay with Alison; a holiday with Anna and Angus in the south of France; a surprise party from Rotary (which included them singing a song written about me); a holiday in Chamonix with Jill and Fraser; and much more. Phew! My treat to myself was the expedition cruise to Antarctica, which would unexpectedly prove to be the start of an amazing journey that led to me fulfilling my dream of becoming a cruise line speaker.

I'm often asked, 'How did you get into cruise line speaking?' Here's how it happened. My friend Nancy had listened to my audiobook on the plane, en route to our meeting point in Santiago before the Antarctica cruise. 'You might have warned me,' she said. 'One minute I was laughing out loud and the next

I was sobbing uncontrollably on the plane.'

A few nights into the cruise, Nancy received an invitation to dinner from Joshua, the future cruise consultant, and I received an invitation to dinner from Duncan, the guest relations manager. This isn't uncommon for solo travellers. We ended up sitting at the same table with another couple. Not surprisingly, we did the usual 'So, what's your name, where are you from and what do you do?' around the table. 'I'm Rhona from Scotland. I'm a retired doctor. I was a consultant forensic psychiatrist working with mentally disordered offenders.' Before I could say any more, Nancy interrupted with, 'And she's an author, her book's called I Don't Talk to Dead Bodies, I read it on the plane and was laughing out loud and then sobbing. It's great, it's very funny. I mean, Chapter 9,' she said with a cheeky grin. We all sat forward, in anticipation. I wrote the book and even I didn't know what was so special about Chapter 9! 'It's called "Tell me about your genitals".' Well, that woke everyone up! We were in the middle of the formal dining room, on a five-star luxury cruise line, but our table had just moved up a gear into party mode. Nancy kept prompting me to tell stories from the book and reminded me of yet another anecdote she'd enjoyed reading. I shared that particular story as requested, and hilarity broke out again.

By this time, we were attracting stares from the other diners. 'She's a great artist, too,' continued Nancy. 'Show them your artwork on your phone.' I passed it around the table, sharing some pointillism and watercolour images. 'She wants to do cruise line speaking and could also run art workshops,' said Nancy. Suddenly, Duncan said, 'I think people would like that. I know the guy who books speakers for the cruise line. Would you like me to contact him?' This would become pivotal moment number two of my retirement journey. Well, that was a no-brainer! Of course I said yes to Duncan. I didn't expect anything to come of it, but true to his word, Duncan contacted his friend and sought me out the next day to share his friend's email address. 'He says to contact him when you get home from the cruise.'

I'd done some research after my book was published and thought I was going to need an agent in order to attract cruise line bookings, but in the email to Duncan's friend I played dumb and said I was interested in cruise line speaking and wondered if he could advise me how to go about it. My initial contact was met with an out-of-office response and the same again at my next attempt. My heart sank. How many times can you contact someone before you become a pest? I didn't care. I was ready to message again but, a few hours later, an email arrived from Duncan's friend, saying that he was 'on the case'. His colleague contacted me a short while after that, offering me two cruises, based purely on Duncan's recommendation. 'Are you free to travel to Japan for two weeks at cherry blossom time, and then Vancouver to Alaska and Japan for three weeks later in the year?' No showreel or references were requested. They obviously had a vacancy and were desperate. But for me, it was good timing. It seemed as if my invitation to dinner with Duncan, and the subsequent connections and opportunities that resulted from our meeting, were serendipitous. There's something about stating your desires, goals or intentions out loud. I believe it makes them more likely to happen.

The term 'manifesting' sounds like one of those slightly out-there, new age-type ideas, but it's really about the power of belief and how we can think a goal into becoming a reality. At one level, it's described as magical thinking, believing that hopes and desires can affect how the world turns. That's a bit too airy-fairy for my somewhat practical head, but I do believe that if you verbalise a goal or plan to others, you'll be more motivated to achieve it. I think the decisions you make after that tend to take you in a direction towards that goal. Your friends may also start making connections for you in support of your journey as a result of having verbalised your goal to them. Verbalising my wishful thinking about becoming a cruise line enrichment lecturer to my publisher and later my cruise buddy Nancy set off a chain reaction of decisions and conversations that hurtled me at pace towards manifesting my goal. That's my version of manifesting and it clearly works for me.

Once I had my first booking, there were practical decisions to be made. Packing for a cruise is always a challenge, but taking on the role of cruise line speaker meant the added pressure of needing five lecturing outfits on top of everything else. Some cruise lines have themed evenings, for example white nights or Caribbean nights, where you're encouraged to wear outfits to match the theme. Then there are the formal nights, the casual nights, the excursion outfits to fit the activity, gym gear (if you need it, but I don't) and swimwear (not for me either). Add in shoes, toiletries and a diffuser hair dryer (I need one for this hair of mine) and it's a pretty full caseload. And being overweight has its additional challenges. My clothes are bigger and therefore need more material, which takes up more space and weighs more. What if they lose my suitcase at the airport? They sell clothes on board most ships but they're not my style and definitely not big enough to fit me. Therefore, as a solo traveller I also need to take a carefully packed piece of hand luggage, containing a mini wardrobe to suit all occasions, just in case. Add in a laptop case when I'm lecturing, and I need a packhorse to get me to and from the airport! If anyone asked 'Are you taking any copies of your book to sell?' the answer would be, 'Absolutely not!' I share the QR code for Amazon as it weighs nothing.

I guess, over time, I'll settle on a smaller wardrobe of items that I know will work on a cruise and then take advantage of the on-board laundry service. A top tip for packing would be to purchase a good quality, colourful suitcase. Mine is black and always more difficult to spot on the luggage carousel. I end up tying coloured scarves around the handle and also use a Rotary luggage strap. When my case eventually appears, I experience a noticeably large exhalation of breath. A two-hour luggage delay in Tampa had me ready to burst into full Shania Twain – that don't impress me much! Airports are my least favourite part of travelling. I always fear I'll end up at the wrong terminal, the wrong departure gate or miss the announcements. Sometimes you aren't able to check in your luggage for a few hours. As a solo traveller, that means crossing your legs as you can't abandon your luggage to go to the toilet. Of course, the opposite problem can arise. It's always possible that you'll be lucky enough to find a toilet somewhere but not be able to work out how to use it.

My first distressing toilet experience was in Beijing airport many years ago. I'd just come off a long-haul flight and needed to go to the bathroom. I opened the door of the cubicle to be confronted by a hole in the floor and a plastic bucket hanging on the back of the door for used toilet paper. There didn't appear to be any toilet paper, either. I was wearing white, cut-off trousers. What was I supposed to do? I guess squat and aim from a height, but I still had no idea what was supposed to happen with my trousers, which would be in the splash zone. No thanks, that's not happening! I emerged quite distressed, with a full bladder. I wasn't the only disgruntled Westerner. A little Chinese lady beckoned me to follow her past a long row of hole-in-the-floor toilets and round the corner. At the end of another row of toilets there was a token Western toilet. Phew!

The whole idea of enrichment lecturing is to provide passengers with a varied programme of entertainment options to act as alternatives to the more physical or interactive on-board activities such as Zumba and trivia. The reason it's called 'enrichment lecturing' is that the topics should be interesting and mentally stimulating, leaving the audience feeling enriched by the experience. What the passengers may not realise is that the opportunity to become a lecturer on a cruise ship is also enriching for the speaker themselves. They get to meet lots of people from different walks of life and visit wonderful destinations, including the exotic toilets!

CHAPTER 23

Konnichiwa (hello)

I like to visit countries where I immediately feel as if I'm entering a different culture, whether it's the traditional costumes, food, customs, language, scenery or architectural style that sets them apart. Japan seemed to tick a lot of those boxes but I'd never actually pursued arranging a trip, even though it had been on my bucket list for years. It was therefore ironic that, as a result of my introduction to cruise line enrichment lecturing, my first assignments would both include Japan. Result! First, I had a two-week tour around Japan, which also included a stop in South Korea. The second was later that year when I was lecturing on a three-week cruise, travelling north from Vancouver to Alaska, then transpacific to Japan. Neither allowed time for a trip on the bullet train, a hike up Mount Fuji or a visit to the snow monkeys, so I might need to return. (Check out the monkeys on YouTube – they're fascinating. They look as if they're lounging in a spa.)

I must confess that the journey to Kobe, where I'd be boarding my ship, was probably the most uncomfortable trip I've ever taken. The cruise line kindly paid for my flight, so it was going to be economy class. I had nothing against this in principle, but I don't have an economy-sized bottom! I'd be taking three flights and embarking the ship the same day, so there was no room for delays or missed connections. That was the most stressful part. Having learned from this experience, I now request to fly the day before and stay overnight in a hotel at the port. At the airport, I asked if I could have an exit seat, as at least I'd be able to stretch my legs (and I have long legs). The situation can also be complicated by my big bottom, which pushes me forward in the seat, meaning that my knees hit the seat in front. When the person in front reclines their seat, there's even less room. It's so uncomfortable! Thankfully, the airline accommodated my request, so I was hoping the 13-hour flight in the middle leg of the journey would be more bearable. Never again! The flight was full, so there would be no changing of seats. Then I discovered that the exit seats don't have an armrest that flips up. Normally, I try to flip them up during the flight or at least allow my bottom to spread under the armrest a little. The exit seats were narrow with rigid sides. I literally didn't fit. My legs started to get pins and needles. I had to alternate sitting awkwardly on one bum cheek at a time, but actually spent a large portion of the flight standing in the ample space in front of my seat watching people sleep in the dark, which sounds a bit creepy!

To complicate matters, the assurances I received at the airport that my case would go right through to my final destination were contradicted by an announcement on the plane. 'Remember to collect all luggage at Osaka and then check it again for your connecting flight and onward travel.' This was inconvenient enough, but I had a fairly quick turnaround between flights, which piled on the stress. When we arrived, we had to go through customs and immigration. The queue was huge, snaking in multiple lines around a large room. I'd worn my light rain jacket, which isn't very breathable, so I started to feel like one of those 'boil-in-the-bag' meals. Then I noticed a sign about making sure you have this specific form and QR code, as indicated on the board. I had neither. There were no staff members available in the vicinity and I couldn't leave my place in the queue. Was I going to be refused entry to Japan after all the trouble and discomfort of getting here *and* miss my first cruise lecturing gig? I thought, 'I'm sweating... They'll think I'm guilty... Maybe they'll think I'm smuggling drugs and pull me aside... I'll miss my connection... I'll miss the ship...' To make matters worse, there were drug sniffer dogs, which always make me feel guilty, despite never having abused drugs in my life. I'm the same when I see a police car on the motorway. I start to feel guilty for no apparent reason. I eventually made it to the front of the queue, having avoided being mistaken for a drug mule. A gracious Japanese gentleman sorted me out with the form and the QR code, and I was off to collect my luggage and check it back in. There was another huge, snaking queue to navigate. This time I really did need help, as the clock was ticking and I was going to miss my connection. I found a member of staff who kindly ushered me to the front of the queue. They looked at my ticket. 'You don't have time to check your luggage here; you'll miss your flight. Take it with you.' They pointed in the direction of an exit, which led to bus transportation to a different terminal. I humped my huge case, hand luggage and laptop bag onto the bus, sweating buckets in my boil-in-the-bag jacket.

I arrived at the other terminal, where I checked the noticeboard. Oh, for goodness sake, there was a change of gate for my flight. It was literally the furthest away. I couldn't have run with all that luggage if you'd paid me a million pounds. I was literally done. I made it to the check-in point for my luggage and into the departure lounge five minutes before they closed the gate. I was exhausted. A short flight later, I arrived at Kobe airport, but still had to get myself to the ship. After collecting my luggage, I exited the baggage collection area and to my surprise I saw a lovely man standing there, holding a sign saying 'MORRISON'. I could've kissed him. And relax...

Ironically, when we arrived at the cruise terminal, I was actually too early for boarding and had to wait before the check-in desk opened. My Rotary luggage strap was still around my suitcase. A voice said, 'A fellow Rotarian?' I turned round to find two smiling American men. The younger man was called Gabriel. We got chatting and agreed that we'd try to organise a Rotary meeting on board, which we did. Seven Rotarians from the UK, USA and Australia met one afternoon to share good practice after I'd asked for it to be announced in the ship's daily newspaper. The cruise director had also announced it in the theatre the evening before, after the show: 'Dr Morrison is going to be busy tomorrow. She has a lecture in the morning, an art class after lunch and a Rotary meeting in the afternoon.'

I regularly saw Gabriel's smiling face around the ship, and on one occasion heard him shout, 'Rhona, do you want to go dancing?' He was dressed in full traditional Japanese attire, an ensemble that included a kimono, *tabi* (white socks separated between the toes) and shoes made of wood, with a raised platform. So, Gabriel and I went to a salsa dance class. Halfway through, he excused himself to change out of his latest purchases and into something that would accommodate his dance moves more easily.

During the cruise, we travelled around Japan and even visited Busan in South Korea. It was such an adventure. Because I was delivering both lectures and pointillism classes for the first time, it's all a bit of a lovely blur of cherry blossom trees, samurai castles, bonsai trees, gardens, sushi restaurants, hot springs, museums, national costumes, temples, tombs, shrines, kimonos, geishas, drummers, fish markets, pirate ships, *torii* gates, Mount Fuji, volcanoes, geothermal activity parks and high-tech toilets! I'd been so determined to see the famous cherry blossom at some point during the trip that I booked all the castle and garden excursions just in case, and it's just as well that I did, as the spectacle doesn't last long. It had come early that year, so we'd missed most of the blossom at the first few ports. The climate changed as we moved north and fortunately we caught the blossom there. People hire national dress to wander among the cherry blossoms for photoshoots. At Lake Ashi, we took a cruise on a 'pirate ship' and a cable car up the mountain to view Mount Fuji from a distance, and also saw the hot springs. The cruise was quite port heavy and I tended to choose the long tours, so it was exhausting, especially when I had to kick into lecturer mode in the morning and artist in the afternoon. I'm not complaining, but it was a bit of a baptism of fire.

I had no idea which cabin I'd been allocated until I arrived on board. To my surprise, when I opened the door to my stateroom, it was enormous, much bigger than anything I'd stayed in before. It soon became clear that I'd been given the cabin for disabled guests. The space would allow for a wheelchair manoeuvring around the room. The bathroom was a large wet room, quite a change from the sometimes cramped shower cubicles I've had, where you dare not drop the soap as there's no room to bend down. If the shower has a curtain rather than a sliding door, you have to ensure that you leave nothing on the floor, as water inevitably escapes under the curtain and floods the bathroom.

As the cruise progressed, a guest entertainer, who was a former West End musical theatre star, boarded the ship at one of the ports. A couple of days later, I met him on the stairs when I was going down to my cabin. I introduced myself as one of the lecturers and said I'd enjoyed his cabaret show. He asked what cabin I was in. 'You're lucky,' he said. 'Someone told me to try to get that one because it's really big. Can I see it to check out the difference?' And so my new pal entered my cabin for a quick look around. I really wish I hadn't washed my large granny pants and hung them up in the shower to dry! As he left after this brief tour (pun intended), my butler came along the corridor. 'Oh no,' I thought, 'I hope they don't start a rumour about me having this random guy in my room!' It's worth remembering that West End stars and other celebrities are just the same as you and me. They still need to wash their underwear and bend over to pick up soap in the shower. I may have been in awe of his talent but he was in awe of my big wetroom!

Japan also caused me some toilet problems, but for completely opposite reasons to China. The toilets were so sophisticated that I couldn't work out how to flush them. They were all slightly different, but featured a whole panel of controls. You can play music, heat the seat, engage a bidet function, play white noise to cancel out the sound of urination or have a rotating plastic cover over the toilet seat. But the basic flush button wasn't obvious. Looking down at the toilet seat and Japanese symbols on the control panel, I was too frightened to push a button and hope for the best for fear that it would be the bidet function! I didn't want to leave it unflushed either, in case someone was waiting outside. Eventually, I stuck my head out of the cubicle and shouted to a member of the entertainment staff, who happened to be on my excursion. They told me to press the blue button. But there wasn't a blue button! After that, I stuck to crossing my legs until I could use the toilet on the ship as that didn't require technical knowledge.

Midway through my first lecturing cruise, I discovered from some of the other lecturers that I could volunteer to escort parties of passengers on shore excursions to assist the local tour guide. Essentially, we were required to herd passengers, walking at the back of the party to ensure that we didn't lose any stragglers en route. It was literally like herding cats. I even got to hold the big wooden lollipop sign showing our excursion number so that passengers could follow me. Each excursion is assigned a difficulty level, which is shared at the time of booking. The higher the rating, the more physical exertion required, for example, walking, climbing stairs or inclines or over uneven surfaces, so you know whether or not it suits your level of mobility. Despite this, there were often elderly passengers who'd disembark the tour bus and ask if they'd have to walk. This is how the conversation would go.

'Do we have far to walk?'

'Yes, quite a bit, this is a walking tour. The bus will come back to pick us up at the meeting point in two hours.'

'Can we just wait here?'

'No, unfortunately the bus is picking us up elsewhere.'

'Just go ahead, we'll follow on slowly.'

'Unfortunately, we all have to enter the park together, as the tour guide is getting tickets for everyone.'

'Is there a toilet?'

'There's a toilet halfway around the park, marked on the map we gave you.'

I'd already advised them to make a toilet stop before we left for the walk to the park! As we neared the pick-up time, I informed people that we needed to head back as the buses couldn't park, so we had to board the bus immediately. However, the stragglers not only stopped to take photos, they also unpacked a bag to look for an enormous photo lens. I issued a polite reminder to move on. Then they took more photos, leaning over a bridge this time, to capture more shots of the cherry blossom. The main tour group had now exited the park gates and was almost out of sight, and I didn't know the way back to the bus pick-up point. Then my camera-laden guests decided to stop at a food truck to buy a hot dog. I nearly blew a gasket, but kept smiling! I was required to carry the cruise line's company backpack, containing a first-aid kit, an accidental injury report form and a toilet roll. It's probably a good thing it didn't contain a weapon because at that point I may have been tempted to use it! There was a major consolation, though, which was that I had the cost of the excursion refunded. I certainly earned my money herding cats, though.

CHAPTER 24

Labour of luck

I was pleased with how my first enrichment lectures had gone down, especially as I had minimal time to prepare them prior to the first cruise. Obviously I was familiar with the content as it was based on my memoir. However, I had to theme five lectures as standalone topics as passengers weren't necessarily going to attend all five. It's still a great surprise to me that anyone wants to attend a lecture on a cruise as there are so many competing activities on board. I settled on the following headings and tried to identify specific anecdotes to link to each theme. The first lecture was going to address the question of why I became a forensic psychiatrist and what it is, because that's a very common question. The rest would cover different patient groups.

1. Frogs and snails and puppy dog tails... What are forensic psychiatrists made of?

This talk is about my journey to becoming a forensic psychiatrist, ready to deal with mentally disordered offenders. Not everyone can deal with someone who may have raped a child or murdered a pensioner. It's not exactly the sort of job you conjure up in your mind while sitting with the career advisor at school.

2. Face to face with murderers...
The human beings behind the headlines

Having assessed hundreds of murderers during my career, I reflected on the more memorable cases, the heartbreak and the lessons learned along the way, including the lady who killed her son and cut out his heart while psychotic.

3. A decade of obsession... Meeting my stalker
and some other tricky situations

What do you do when a patient brings a machete to the clinic or you discover that you have a stalker? In this talk, I share these and other amusing anecdotes of tricky situations along the way. There's no shortage of material.

4. Don't mention bananas...
This job is not for everyone

Working with sex offenders can be challenging. I share situations where I dealt with mentally disordered sex offenders and some uncomfortable encounters in the outpatient department, including the offender who dropped his trousers and started masturbating in my office mid-assessment!

5. Girls behind bars... A life sentence

This includes tales of the challenges of working as a psychiatrist in a female prison. I served more than a life sentence, but I got to go home at night. This was probably the most difficult subject matter for me. There weren't so many funny stories as it was all about self-harm and trauma. I did, however, include the story of a female prisoner convicted of murder who sold me a car while she was on a pre-release work placement. I had to give her my home address to complete the purchase.

This was all new for me as I had to get to know the requirements of sound and lighting, plus the projection of my PowerPoint onto the big screen. For only the second time, I had to use a head mic, the first having been at my book launch. It was a bit stressful having to ensure that the timing of the lectures was approximately 45 minutes and not more than an hour, so that the ship's entertainment schedule was adhered to. I was concerned that I'd either have too much or too little material and wanted to ensure that the underlying message about destigmatisation of mental illness stayed intact, while including some bizarre, scary, humorous and thought-provoking content. No pressure!

The short timescale between my first bookings as an enrichment lecturer and actually having to format five lectures and prepare all the paperwork for entering Japan meant that my PowerPoints were pretty much non-existent. I couldn't just print pictures off the internet in case of copyright infringement, so I'm sure I would've been marked down for that in my feedback. Registering with Adobe months later meant that I had legitimate access to images, so subsequent lectures had more engaging visuals, and they'll no doubt continue to evolve.

At the end of each lecture, I'd always say that I was happy to chat, as the option of a roving microphone doesn't work well in a large, three-tier theatre. For example, on the five-star cruise, it was mostly 'How did you cope with all of that?', but on bigger ships, the topics were varied and interesting and sometimes quite unexpected. For example, 'If someone becomes a 35-year-old transvestite, do you think he's mentally ill?' My response was, 'Being a transvestite is not a symptom of major mental illness. Did you have someone particular in mind?' It was their own son. What do you say to that?

A therapist in the audience said, 'I look after veterans with PTSD, so I'm pleased that you made the point about being mindful regarding context and not judging people.' I was pleased that the content resonated with them. I wasn't expecting this one, though: 'My school friend murdered someone and decapitated them. Do you think I should visit him in the penitentiary?' And another man said, 'I've had a traumatic brain injury and have balance issues that make me look drunk. Thank you for asking people not to be judgemental.' He subsequently came along to my pointillism art class. His manual dexterity was impaired, but he felt safe enough not to be judged and took part. I was delighted. One lady was on her first solo cruise after losing her husband. She said my talks about what I'd achieved since Richard died gave her hope. She just needed a hug, so that's what she got.

Each time I deliver my lectures, I hone them a little more, getting a sense of what engages the audience, what gets a gasp or a laugh and what generates discussion afterwards. It's amazing what people take away from the content, and it isn't always what I'd anticipated. In my attempt to explain the techniques and strategies I use when trying to elicit information from a reluctant offender, several audience members approached me afterwards to say that they'd learned techniques that would be useful for their work in retail and the financial sector. Who knew? A lot of my work involved taking the time to get to know people and asking what mattered to them, building trust, not judging them or making assumptions. I wonder if that resonates with you, as it's applicable in all walks of life.

It makes me glow inside when passengers accost me on the ship, in the lift, toilet, dining room and even on the tour bus and say, 'I'm loving your talks... So interesting... When's the next one, Doc?' A foster carer from Australia approached me once, bravely sharing a very difficult situation that she was dealing with back home, involving major mental illness, a stalker and someone threatening suicide. She said, 'People need to hear your message. I wish you'd come to Australia to talk.' My response was, 'If someone pays for my flight, I'll be there.' I'll chalk that up as a success, knowing that one more person may have left feeling supported, understood or with their mindset challenged. Changing attitudes and culture happens one person at a time, but that can generate discussion with others and then a ripple becomes a wave of change.

My performances weren't without their issues, though. Sometimes the time printed in the ship's newspaper didn't marry up with the lecture slot I'd been given or the lecture didn't appear on the schedule at all. On one ship, they advertised lecture number one, saying it was about forensic science, dead bodies and scenes of crime, the complete opposite of what I was going to be talking about! A quick chat with the entertainment staff and these matters were resolved. On another occasion, the orchestra came onto the stage behind the screen where my PowerPoint was displayed and started warming up while I was still talking! This resulted in some angry stage crew and passengers, but I had to keep on talking. Lecturers are clearly told that if the tech doesn't work, they've just got to keep going. It's also nice to be able to watch other speakers and performers in action as it's an opportunity to learn from them and hone my skills. On one occasion, I attended a comedy show and the comedian had the same experience with the orchestra that I did, so at least I didn't feel it was directed at me!

Before I travelled on the first cruise, I offered to deliver art workshops on board as well, but was told I was only being booked as an enrichment lecturer. However, once on board, I met the assistant cruise director and showed them examples of my pointillism pen-and-ink animal images, and they were impressed enough to let me run art workshops as well. I taught pointillism and drew themed images, for example Japanese dolls, koi carp and cherry blossoms. However, to practise the technique of making pictures using dots, we started with a simple egg. I created a worksheet that looked a bit like a 'painting by numbers' egg, although instead of numbers corresponding with different colours of oil paint, they related to a grid with different concentrations of dots. Because I'd be providing the pre-made templates of the images the participants needed, it was advertised as 'art for all', no skill required. If you could hold a pen and make a dot of ink on the page, you were in.

I asked the assistant cruise director how many people were likely to show up for an art class on a ship with only 400 passengers. Going on past experience, she said six to 12. I had enough fine-liner pens with me for about 20 people, so all we needed to do was make photocopies of the templates plus the final pointillism drawings that I'd prepared for them to copy. When I entered the room ten minutes before the start time, there was no one there. There was still no one there ten minutes later. I felt quite downhearted, but didn't realise I'd entered via the rear entrance of the venue, which was nearest to my cabin. The assistant cruise director arrived and told me there was quite a queue outside. When we opened the doors, 46 people poured in, eager to find out about pointillism and how to do it. Staff were quickly dispatched to locate more pens and photocopy more sheets. In the meantime, I was able to demonstrate the technique and tell them about it while we waited for the equipment to arrive. At the next port of call, some of the entertainment staff were tasked with finding a stationery store from which to buy even more fine-liner pens. Each time I ran the workshop, large numbers of passengers turned up to attempt the next image I'd created for them. I found myself sitting in my cabin late at night creating the material for yet another workshop.

Passengers who weren't remotely arty gave it a try. It had quite a powerful effect on one gentleman in particular. I'd explained that it was almost like painting by numbers. Once you'd identified an area that needed a particular concentration of dots, you could just dot away without having to think about it. The darker the area on the picture, the more dots were required. It's almost like a mindfulness exercise, as it encourages you to focus in the moment, shut out your worries and feel calm. Passengers became so engrossed in repetitive dotting that they zoned out from everything else. The gentleman in question wasn't engaging in any banter with fellow passengers. He was totally focused on creating his picture and said, 'I feel quite sleepy.' His wife said, 'He never sits still at home for more than five minutes. He's always finding a task that needs doing, even if there aren't any. I've never seen him sit in one spot for so long.' Later that day, I met the cruise director, who said, 'I've just been approached by a man in the corridor who wanted to show me his picture of a koi carp. He was really delighted with it.' I knew exactly who he meant.

What I learned from the Japanese trip, in addition to the intricacies of respectful bowing to elders and the difference between sushi and sashimi, was that I love solo travelling and actually enjoy it more when I'm working. I enjoyed the lecturing, but I knew it would become easier as I refined my material and sorted out the PowerPoint.

People say I'm lucky, and of course I am, but I made this luck happen. I studied and worked hard for nearly 40 years to learn my craft, had to cope with losing Richard when I retired, started an art business and wrote a book. All these experiences led me down a path where I had the foundations in place to allow me to pursue my dream retirement job as a cruise line enrichment lecturer. I believe everyone can make their own luck. When you set yourself a goal, you start making decisions and choices that are more likely to deliver you to your desired destination.

CHAPTER 25

Rock around the clock

With one experience of enrichment lecturing under my belt, I felt better equipped to deal with my second, although this time it was on a three-week cruise with a transpacific crossing and lots of sea days. I'd never done that sort of thing before, and certainly not as a solo traveller. I wondered how I'd cope with all that time on my own. This time I'd be flying into Vancouver, so I arranged to travel a couple of days early. Last time I was in Vancouver, Fraser was a young boy and he collapsed with acute abdominal pain. Our time in the city, pre-Alaskan cruise, was then spent in A&E. Richard panicked, trying to find a working telephone to call the insurance company, terrified that Fraser had a ruptured appendix and would need an operation. Fortunately, it was nothing too serious. The insurance covered it and we made it to the cruise the next day. Needless to say, we never got to see Vancouver.

My godfather is in his nineties and his son Alan lives in Vancouver. We hadn't seen each other for decades, so we arranged to meet. He works for the port authority, managing the IT for all the ship pilots who guide cruise ships in and out of port. We'd be needing his colleague's services when we set sail. I also managed a trip to Stanley Park and, to avoid getting lost, opted for a horse and carriage tour. For dinner, I walked two blocks to a restaurant recommended by the hotel. My heart was pounding and I kept looking behind me to make sure no one was following me. I don't think I've ever properly got over being jumped by a group of teenage boys when I was at school. I rarely venture out on my own in big cities. I also arranged a trip to the VanDusen Botanical Garden before it was time to board the ship. My solo traveller confidence was growing, little by little. I won't wander the streets as I quickly feel vulnerable and lost, but a taxi ride to a specific venue or a paid excursion are now on my list of things I feel comfortable doing.

We'd be cruising north to visit well-known haunts in Alaska, some of which I'd visited years earlier with the family. This time, I was planning to tick off one of my bucket list items, which we couldn't afford to choose as an excursion for a family of four all those years before. I wanted to see a big black bear in the wild, scooping a salmon from the river and eating it for lunch. With wildlife there are no guarantees, but I was hopeful. Do you have a bucket list? People often talk about having bucket list items but don't actually make an attempt to tick them off. What's stopping you and can you overcome it?

When I boarded the ship, I had an immediate feeling of familiarity as I'd been on the same one in Japan earlier in the year. The assistant cruise director met me as I collected my cruise card. He remembered me. 'Will you be doing art workshops this time as well?' I guess that was my query answered before I'd had a chance to ask it. The ship was repositioning back to Japan for the next season, hence the transpacific crossing.

I was amazed by how many friendly Australians were on board. I met a lovely group of solo travellers and quickly made friends and dinner companions. I met two fellow authors and have kept in touch with Kathy and Jeanette ever since. My friendship with Jeanette was unexpected. I'd missed the first team trivia session because of a meeting with the assistant cruise director. People stay in the same teams for the whole cruise, so it looked as if I'd missed out. I went down on the second day, but the teams were all full. There was a small, grey-haired lady, dressed all in black, who appeared to be doing the quiz on her own at a separate table. I wondered if she was a solo traveller too, so I approached her and started a conversation. Our team of stragglers eventually grew until we had more than the maximum number of participants allowed for a trivia team, but we didn't care. They shouldn't have included me in the numbers anyway, as I'm absolutely rubbish at general knowledge and even worse at the medical questions, which is worrying! Who needs to know how many bones are in the human body anyway?!

Jeanette had a fascinating history. She was an accomplished artist and also in the middle of writing a book. On the surface we weren't people you'd instantly put together. She seemed quiet and reserved and I'm a brightly coloured, chatty extrovert. Somehow, we just hit it off. We'd sit together at solo traveller get-togethers, put the world to rights, decide where we fancied eating, then see if anyone wanted to join us. She came to my art classes and lectures as well. We had a lot in common and the conversation was rich and varied. I'd found another cruise buddy. Two years on, I took delivery of her published book and she's been in contact to say she may visit me in Scotland.

In Ketchikan, I took a walk and visited a salmon leap before boarding a bus tour that would take me on an excursion out into the wilderness. First, we had a two-hour scenic boat journey before arriving at a remote fish farm, then a long walk through the forest took us to a lookout spot where black bears are sometimes seen in the wild. Our luck was in! For 45 minutes, we were mesmerised by a large black bear wading through rocks in fairly shallow water, catching salmon as they leapt out of the water. What I wasn't expecting was to see him hold the salmon down against the rock, secured by two enormous, clawed paws, then bite into it, only to throw it half eaten back into the water. The guide explained that the bears prefer the female salmon as they're coming into spawn, and they love the taste of the fish eggs. If they catch a male salmon, they often throw it back into the water and try to catch a female one instead.

I was travelling alone on this excursion, but as usual I'd started talking to a random lady at the bus stop before the tour bus arrived. Her name was Lisa and she was having a day out on her own as her husband and friends were on an all-day fishing expedition. She asked if she could sit with me on the boat and we shared our stories, as you do with perfect strangers! She took my contact details before we left and still kindly follows my Facebook page. She wasn't a cruise passenger, but she's still a buddy acquired while cruising.

Meeting Lisa reminded me of a similar experience I had while on holiday in Tenerife with Jill in the summer of 2019. We found ourselves at a bus stop early one morning, waiting to board a tour bus. There were four other people waiting and, just like her mum would do, Jill struck up a conversation.

'Are you going on a tour too?'

'Yes.'

'Where are you from?' She'd recognised their accents.

'Gourock, in Scotland.'

'We're from Cumbernauld.'

'What do you do there?'

'I'm a prison officer and my mum was a forensic psychiatrist, but now she's got an art business. She does pet portraits.'

As Jill uttered those words, she had her phone out, proudly showing them examples of my artwork and urging me to give them one of my business cards. Since then she's gone on to become a one-woman promotion team, forever contacting me to say, 'I sold another book at work. Can you talk to someone about your book as they're writing one? Could you do some calligraphy place names for a wedding? I said you wouldn't mind. Can you do a pointillism picture of the prison? Someone special is retiring. Somebody's going to contact you about a pet portrait. Someone at work has problems with their child. Do you mind meeting to have a chat? I said you wouldn't mind.' She's a born helper with a heart of gold.

Fast-forward several months and I received an email from a man I didn't know, saying, 'You might not remember me, but we met at a bus stop in Tenerife. I wonder if you're still doing pet portraits?' I was, so I agreed to do a watercolour painting of a dog. He agreed to come to collect it with his wife and grandchildren. Fortunately, they were delighted with it, and we had a proper introduction over some tea and biscuits.

A few years after the pet portrait request, another email arrived. 'Remember me? We met at a bus stop in Tenerife. I hear that you're a Rotarian and you do talks. I'm the president of our local club and I wondered if you'd like to come and talk?' I must have done about 60 talks on Zoom, from the Isle of Wight to Stornoway and everywhere in between, all word-of-mouth referrals from one Rotary Club to the next. We were now able to meet face to face, so I'd be heading to Gourock. He insisted that I go to his house beforehand to meet up with all four of those people from the bus stop in Tenerife, so we had tea and cake before my talk. Wouldn't it be funny if Lisa emailed me out of the blue looking for a pet portrait? Stranger things have happened. 'Hello, we met at a bus stop in Ketchikan...' What is it with me and bus stops!?

Anyway, back to Alaska. The next stop was Juneau, where I'd arranged a trip to the Mendenhall Glacier and then the Gold Belt Tram, which would take us up to the viewpoint that looked down over the harbour and surrounding mountains. At the top of the mountain there was a craftsman carving a new totem pole. The towns in Alaska looked like something out of the Wild West, with painted wooden buildings, some built on stilts out in the water. The air was clean and crisp and I even spotted a bald eagle posing on top of a telegraph pole.

I'd booked another boat trip at the next port to explore the wilderness. We spotted wild bears on the distant shoreline and salmon leaping out of the water before arriving at a remote lodge at the water's edge and eating s'mores around a campfire. There were bear claw marks on the bark of the surrounding trees. Next, we visited a bear sanctuary. Bears are such a problem in the area that if an orphaned bear is rescued, it can't be re-released into the wild. The sanctuary we visited had a collection of large, mature bears who were in a huge enclosure. We got pretty close, so I can definitely remove bears from my bucket list.

Back on board, I'd been asked to run pointillism art classes on sea days as well as deliver my lectures, so I was busy. I decided to create images linked to this specific cruise, so I spent a few hours late into the night sitting in my stateroom, creating material for the next class. A big bear and a sea otter were added to the collection. The other lecturers on board were quite a diverse group. We had experts on gut microbiomes, artificial intelligence and the British Empire, as well as a destination lecturer. With each of us delivering five different lectures, there were plenty of lectures to choose from. Sea days certainly had a multitude of intellectual options on the activity list as well as the swimming pool, spa, trivia and entertainment alternatives.

At the next port, I took a boat trip with my new cruise buddy, Kathy. We spotted sea otters and lots of very noisy, rather smelly harbour seals. On board the small boat, I met a real crusty sea dog character who turned out to be an Alaskan Rotarian. What are the chances of that? Next, we were off to Dutch Harbor in Unalaska. I thought they'd made a mistake with the name, but apparently that's what it's called. It was so remote. Dutch Harbor is on Amaknak Island, where there was a famous battle in 1942. It was one of the few places in the United States to be bombarded by a foreign power during the Second World War. Captain Cook visited before that in 1778, en route to the

Northwest Passage. That's the end of your history lesson, just in case any of this comes up in a trivia quiz! Now it's famous for an American TV programme called *The Deadliest Catch*, which is a reality show following crab fishers aboard their vessels in the Bering Sea as they attempt to catch giant Alaskan king crabs. There are often fatalities, so it's not an occupation for the faint hearted. We visited the tiny local museum and church, having been driven there in a steamed-up yellow school bus. It wasn't really set up for tourists. Planned stops in Unalaska are often cancelled due to bad weather, so we were lucky to have visited at all.

Back on board, we faced several days at sea while crossing the Pacific Ocean to Japan. The ship's clocks were changing an hour per day to adjust to the different time zones. One day, I went to bed on the 15th and woke up on the 17th! We'd crossed the international date line and lost a day. That really scrambled my brain. Just as well it wasn't my birthday on the 16th! However, it was my book's first birthday during our sea days, so I had a special 'book birthday party' dinner with some new cruise buddies, and the chef piped 'Happy birthday' on my dessert plate. Another photo op for Facebook! The sea days were a bit of a blur of lectures, art classes, entertainment and eating. One evening, the Indian chef even made me and my solo traveller friends a special banquet of our choosing. On another night, we cooked our own food on hot lava stones out on deck, with space heaters and blankets to keep us warm. The vast darkness of the sky and sea enveloped us, only to be interrupted by the white horses capping the waves of the turbulent ocean as we looked out to sea from the deck. We definitely experienced a bit of a swell out in the open water.

During the day, the executive chef did a cookery demo, showing passengers how to make the perfect risotto. He was Scottish so, after the demo, I felt emboldened and approached my fellow countryman to ask if he'd be willing to make a cupcake for me, decorated with male genitals made of marzipan. It was to be used as a prop for my sex offender talk, during which I tell the story about my retirement cupcakes. 'I could, but I don't think I'd be allowed,' was his reply. I'd have to improvise.

The next day, before my lecture, I placed a plate with a banana and a muffin from the breakfast buffet in the sound booth, ready for collection when it was time to put on my head mic. When I arrived, there was no muffin. 'Where's my muffin, Pablo?' I asked the sound man. 'I ate it!' was his reply. So, I no longer had an adequate prop as a humorous interlude during what can be fairly heavy subject matter. I'd planned to hold it up and remove half of the cake wrapper, raise it to my mouth, shake my head and say, 'No... What did they expect me to do with that?' I kept in the story and told them what I'd hoped to do, but that Pablo ate the muffin. That got a laugh, anyway. More recently I purchased two stress toys that are shaped like a banana and a cupcake, so I now have permanent, non-perishable, non-edible props for future cruises.

We eventually arrived in Japan. In Kushiro, we visited a volcano with sulphur gases emerging from yellow-stained holes in the rock, then an *onsen* (a hot spring). We'd been given a towel as we left the ship for the excursion, and the guide told us on the bus that it was compulsory to bathe naked. OMG! That's not happening! What have I booked?! Fortunately, we just rolled up our trousers and had a foot spa in the geothermally heated waters, so naked bathing wasn't required. Lunch was included. The tiny, tapas-type dishes the Japanese produce are a work of art in themselves, all brightly coloured with intricate shapes and designs. I must confess that I'm not really a fan of sushi, sashimi, bean curd or fermented anything. We even came across an advert for 100-year-old eggs at the top of the volcano, and I gave them a miss as well.

My excursion at the next port took me to what I can only describe as a Japanese theme park, with lots of actors in traditional geisha and samurai soldier outfits, performing in stage shows, doing fighting demos and posing for photos.

All this was happening among beautifully manicured gardens with bonsai trees. I managed to get a selfie with a geisha and a samurai. It had to be done.

Our last stop was Osaka, where I managed to book an excursion to Tokyo. Here we saw high-rise, high-end shops, bonsai gardens, national monuments, a palace, a famous shrine, a rickshaw and lots of people in traditional kimonos. The sight of two sumo wrestlers crossing at the traffic lights, with their familiar chunky build and topknot hairstyles, was something you don't see in Glasgow on a regular Saturday.

Towards the end of the cruise, I was in the lounge one evening when in walked Joshua, the future cruise consultant from my Antarctica cruise earlier in the year. He was the one who'd been present at the dinner when Duncan had offered to connect me with the man who booked cruise line lecturers. I'd never been able to thank him for triggering the chain of events that brought me my first booking. We recognised each other right away. A welcome hug was followed by a chance to share an update on what had happened as a result of that famous 'tell me about your genitals' dinner in Antarctica. We took a selfie to send to Duncan, which allowed me to thank him for playing such a pivotal role in my lecturing journey. It really is a small world.

CHAPTER 26

Murder on the barge

While I was away at sea, I received two pretty special messages. First, I heard back from the Global Book Awards that I'd won the gold medal for my genre. I was shocked and delighted. Now I can actually say that I'm an award-winning author! The advert for the competition had popped into my email a short while before the anniversary of my publication date and I thought, 'Why not?' The second message was from my publisher to say that their foreign rights department had sold the rights to my book to a Taiwanese publisher. My book is going to be published in Chinese. Woo hoo! I wonder if the key message in my book will translate into a different language. Even though I won't be able to read it, I look forward to having a copy of the Chinese version on my bookshelf!

Since the book launch, I've actively sought out opportunities to continue talking about my book on radio shows and podcasts, as well as giving talks in libraries, colleges and universities. In 2023, I became aware of Scottish Book Week. So, my specific referral request at BNI was for my colleagues to visit their local libraries and ask if they'd like to host a free

Meet the Author event. I gave them a summary sheet about me and my book and got three bookings. Result! I advertised the talks on my Facebook page and each library advertised on the premises and on their social media pages. Apparently, they were delighted to have me for Scottish Book Week. Approximately 20 people turned up at each event and I spoke for about an hour, followed by a question and answer session and book signing.

Two standout things happened at these events. At one, there was a man in the front row with a guide dog. He spoke to me at the end to say how much he'd enjoyed the talk but that he wouldn't be queuing up to buy a book as he was blind. I felt so pleased to be able to tell him that I'd recorded an audiobook. To be honest, I recorded it so that my mum, who's visually impaired, could listen to the book, and hadn't really considered a wider audience in terms of disability and inclusion. That same night, a young man waited patiently in the queue and was the last person to come up to the desk. My daughter Jill had kindly been dealing with book sales, which allowed me time to sign books and chat to people. The young man said, 'Thank you, that really helped.' I wasn't sure what I'd said or done that had been so helpful, but it became clearer when he added, 'My brother killed two of my family members when he was psychotic.' I wasn't expecting that. I always try to encourage people not to be judgemental. The person who has offended due to mental illness didn't ask to be ill and often won't realise that what they were doing was wrong, as it was in response to symptoms that they believed to be real at the time, for example, command auditory hallucinations or paranoid delusions. I also talk about the impact on families and how the newspaper reporting of incidents can be stigmatising for all of them. The ripple effect after the incident can be significant. I seemed to have struck a chord with this young man. Acknowledging these issues appeared to have lifted a weight off him. What a burden to have to carry around, feeling guilty by association.

When I spoke at another library, one lady became visibly upset. Later, she disclosed to the whole group during a Q&A session that she'd also had a stalker. She felt so relieved after I talked about my stalker and how I dealt with the situation that she now felt hope that she too might be able to move on. Her experience was very distressing to listen to. I was fortunate to have had the support of the NHS, the police, the Medical Defence Union lawyers and the courts behind me when I was dealing with my stalker.

These were not the only talks I gave during Scottish Book Week. Some months earlier, I'd visited the William Patrick Library in Kirkintilloch. I used to go there with my mum when I was at primary school and needed information for a school project. I tentatively approached the desk and spoke to the librarian. 'I'm a local author and wondered if it would be possible to have my book stocked in the library?' The answer was yes, and all I had to do was give them a copy. Well, that was easy. I handed over a signed copy and asked if they'd be interested in a free Meet the Author event. The librarian said their book club would probably like that and told me that someone would contact me. Some weeks later, when I thought they'd forgotten, I received an email and the talk was arranged. On the day, a lady arrived and introduced herself as being a member of the book club. She said, 'I've got something for you, Dr Morrison,' and handed over a heavy carrier bag. She looked on expectantly as I delved into the bag. There was a bottle of Irn-Bru, a packet of KitKat biscuits and a carefully wrapped pile of homemade egg mayonnaise sandwiches on an assortment of different breads. To a casual onlooker, this would've seemed totally bizarre, but the unwritten message to me was that she'd read my book. I'd spent most of my career zooming about in my car from the hospital to the community outpatient clinic, to my office, to management meetings, to police stations, to the court, to patients' homes and so on. Swigging Irn-Bru and eating chunky KitKats and egg mayo sandwiches in the car was my regular routine. Colleagues didn't have to ask what I wanted at the shop for lunch as it was the same every day. I'd reported this in my book, so here was this lady saying, 'I thought I'd bring you some lunch.' How thoughtful and meaningful.

The talk went well. The library contacted me afterwards to thank me and said they'd pass on my details to other libraries in the area. The sandwich lady also gave me a card, which was another thoughtful addition. She said, 'It's not factually accurate, but I thought you'd like it.' It was a postcard of a penguin and a polar bear holding a can of Irn-Bru with icebergs behind them. She'd obviously been following me on Facebook, where I talked about my travels in Antarctica. There are penguins in Antarctica, but polar bears are only found in the Arctic. Another useful fact for a trivia quiz!

Months went by before I heard from the council that runs all the libraries in the area. One of their other libraries wanted me to participate in an event for Scottish Book Week but the library had closed temporarily due to a building issue. Instead, they'd chartered a canal boat and planned to host an event on that instead. I'd be one of two authors doing a Q&A. The other was Scottish crime writer Allan Martin. We arranged a planning meeting and the idea of 'murder on the barge' took shape. It would be crime fiction meets crime fact. Sadly our time on the barge was limited by funding constraints, so it felt a little bit rushed, but what a fun idea.

If every person who hears me talk tells one other person, the destigmatisation message will spread. I love it when family members send me screenshots of Facebook messages from friends saying, 'Guess what my mum is reading... She loves it.' When photos arrive from abroad, that makes my heart sing, as it means my message is spreading far and wide.

More recently, I've been added to the Probus speaker circuit. This is an organisation based around friendship, fellowship and having fun in retirement. It's predominantly made up of retired older men. They regularly invite speakers, so I'm happy to oblige them or other organisations for free. I was also approached by a charity to ask if I'd speak at their event. They run a community cafe and a food bank and provide new home starter kits. I wasn't sure how a talk from me was relevant to their organisation or how it would go down, but they said they'd advertise it, so all I had to do was turn up. The week before, they contacted me to say that they'd had to ticket the event, as the response had been overwhelming. They'd capped it at 50, the capacity for the room. Wow. I arrived early for a chat and a tour of the impressive facility. I was keen to ensure that I chose my subject matter carefully as the charity was located in the area where I used to work. I checked the list of attendees and didn't recognise any names, but while I was watching people filing into the hall I kept hearing people say, 'Oh, do I need a ticket? I haven't got one.' They let a few extras slip in, so it was standing room only at the back of the hall. The next person without a ticket was very familiar to me. It was one of my former patients, who was on my caseload for years and one of my biggest successes. At one point he had an undiagnosed psychotic illness but eventually responded well to treatment. He was the one who'd dropped his trousers and masturbated in my office. I was honoured to have him in the audience and gifted him a free book afterwards, but it was important to be discreet and not let anyone else know he was once my patient. Some old nursing and criminal justice social work colleagues and a new psychiatrist in the area also popped in to see me.

You just never know who'll be in the audience and what stories will resonate with them. For example, two people contacted me to talk about the chapter about my research into blood pressure and Down's syndrome. I didn't think that would be of much interest to anyone, but as it was the only research I ever had published while I was a doctor, I felt I needed to include it. I guess it was my attempt at challenging my own insecurities. Once I eventually recognised and valued my own training, experience and practical clinical skills, I was happier in my own skin, but it didn't stop me feeling the need to add something a little academic to the book. There's that imposter syndrome again.

Lauren, who typed the first draft of my memoir, was impacted by this chapter because her brother has Down's syndrome. Several years later, Lorraine from my business group had quite a dramatic response to the chapter. Her teenage son has Down's syndrome, and when she read my book, he'd recently transitioned from children's to adults' cardiology services. People with Down's syndrome often have cardiac abnormalities. Her son had cardiac problems and was on several medications. He'd been fairly stable and asymptomatic, but when he transitioned to the adult service they'd been concerned about his low blood pressure and started messing about with his medication. When Lorraine read my chapter on low blood pressure and Down's syndrome, she went straight to the internet, printed off my original research paper and presented it to the hospital consultant. As a result, her son's medication was changed back to his previous prescription. That was certainly an unintended consequence of my book. He made me a lovely gift as a thank you. To my surprise, I recently found out that my friend Anne, who was a learning disability consultant psychiatrist, used my research findings to inform management of blood pressure in Down's syndrome as well.

When I eventually said goodbye to BNI in 2024, they organised a leaving cake featuring the front cover of my book. I was overwhelmed by the kind words and generous theatre vouchers, cake, flowers and gifts. Between them, over the years, my BNI colleagues had secured me Meet the Author events in multiple libraries, lots of book sales, lots of art commissions, multiple art merchandise purchases, found several shops and cafes to sell my art, got me lecturing gigs, a newspaper article, several radio shows and podcasts. Brilliant. This lovely group of people also got me through a solitary pandemic, with weekly

Zoom meetings and quiz nights. We also held murder mystery nights to keep us amused and our spirits up. I dressed up as a chef, a policeman and various other dodgy characters. Paul dressed as a monk in robes and a giant cross. His message on the Zoom chat when he went to fill up his glass was 'Gone to feed the orphan boys.' And, when giving clues, he delivered them in a monk-like chant. Hilarious! It was a lot of fun, but it's the friendships I made at BNI that stand out.

CHAPTER 27

Call my agent

My first two cruise line lecturing gigs came about in a fortuitous manner, but it became clear that I'd need to find an agent to access other cruise lines. Cuddy, an acquaintance I'd made through my business group, used to be a cruise line entertainment director. He'd heard me speak at my BNI business group, interviewed me on his podcast and also commissioned a painting from me. He wrote to his old cruise line and said, 'You should have this woman on your world cruise because she can lecture and run art workshops for you.' How kind is that? The cruise line subsequently pointed me towards the talent agency they use and I contacted them right away. The agent was looking for a showreel, but I didn't have one. I was going to have to engage a videographer. Fortunately, I knew Katy via my business group, and she was extremely helpful. She recorded me talking at home in front of a green screen and was able to add text, music and photographs behind me. I also needed footage of me lecturing, so I asked my business group colleagues if they'd mind waiting behind after our weekly meeting so I could record a snippet of a lecture. I chose to share my stalker story. After I'd submitted the showreel and was accepted onto the agency's list of enrichment lecturers, I had access to a private Facebook group for everyone who'd been signed by them. Many of the specialist enrichment lecturer opportunities had already been taken for 2024, but I signed up for four trips with the cruise line that my friend used to work for. I'd be transitioning from a 500-passenger ship to a 2,500-passenger ship with a much bigger auditorium. I'd also be competing with sunbathing in 30-degree temperatures and all the other scheduled ship activities, including the buffet, the pool, the bar, the spa, the casino, dance classes, movies, trivia quizzes and bingo. I know what I'd choose, and it's not the lecture! Did I ever imagine I'd be saying, 'I'll just have to call my agent in Florida'? No!

My first four bookings were as follows: Tampa, Florida to Los Angeles (via the Panama Canal); Galveston, Texas to Barcelona (transatlantic); Southampton to Rome (Mediterranean); and a round trip from Galveston via the southern Caribbean. Sadly, the Southampton to Rome cruise was subsequently cancelled, but within a day I had an alternative booking to travel from Seattle to Tokyo (transpacific). It was all very exciting. The cruise line would fund the flights and the cruise (in a guest cabin), but I'd be paying for my excursions, internet and drinks packages and also pay the agent a nightly fee. The amount would vary according to the cruise line, with luxury cruises costing the speaker a little bit more, but still at a fraction of the cost of the overall cruise, which for me would also have had a single-person supplement.

Embarking on the first lecturing cruise booked via my agent was quite a poignant moment for me. This was the cruise itinerary that Richard had wanted to take but never got to experience. I was doing this one for him. As an engineer, he was always keen to visit large structural engineering projects such as the Falkirk Wheel in Scotland and the Three Gorges Dam in China. The Panama Canal was also on his list. I'd been to Florida, LA and Mexico before, but I'd be visiting Guatemala, Panama and Colombia for the first time.

Colombia has a reputation for organised crime, violence, homicide, extortion, robbery and kidnapping, but that wasn't my experience. It was really lovely visiting the old town of Cartagena with its colourful buildings and ornate balconies, and seeing the ladies dressed like Carmen Miranda, balancing baskets of fruit on their heads for the tourists. When I asked if I could take a photo of them, I suddenly found a basket of fruit being placed on my head, so I was going to be in the photo too! Back at the ship, we discovered we were moored next to a free zoo, where we saw peacocks, anteaters, sloths and monkeys up close, with parrots landing on our heads. It was a great day all round.

Next, we were off to Colón in Panama, where I'd booked an excursion on a small, six-seater boat to see wild monkeys on an island. The boat operator regularly stopped at the same spot, so when he produced some fresh fruit, monkeys appeared in the trees near the shoreline, ready to enjoy their lunch. One even jumped onto our boat. En route, we found ourselves dwarfed by a container ship transporting hundreds of large metal storage containers. It felt quite daunting. Then we were off to navigate the locks of the Panama Canal. It took eight hours to pass through the canal, with barely a few inches either side between us and the side wall of each lock. I don't think I would've understood the mechanism had I not been on the Falkirk Wheel, which is a unique carousel for canal boats that lifts one boat at a time from one level to another. I did receive a certificate for travelling through the Panama Canal, though. As a feat of engineering, it's astonishing. We watched the walls of the channel as we sat eating dinner. All we could see was stone outside the window.

In Guatemala, I took a tour to Antigua, which is surrounded by volcanoes. On a long bus ride through the countryside, we saw lots of tin-roofed stalls by the roadside selling fresh fruit. It appeared quite run down and deprived. We'd occasionally pass ornately decorated buses, which seemed quite out of place, but we eventually arrived in the old town with its colonial-style buildings. Several had been destroyed by earthquakes and volcanic disturbances. There were plenty of street vendors with bales of brightly coloured cloth balanced precariously on their heads and baskets full of handmade crafts. On our walking tour of the square and town centre, we were pursued by the vendors every step of the way. We also visited a chocolate factory, where we learned the history of chocolate and had a chocolate-making workshop. Later on, the chocolates we'd made were delivered to our bus for us to take back to the ship. It was really hot and they were starting to melt, so I had to eat them all. There was nothing else for it!

When we arrived in Puerto Vallarta in Mexico, I took an excursion to a ranch, where we'd be making traditional Mexican dishes for our lunch, including *mole*, a sauce made from lots of fibre, chillis, nuts and seeds. I was in the team making the *mole*. We fed the leftover scraps to goats in the field. En route, we stopped off to visit a traditional tortilla factory and took a tour of a church in a local village. It would've been rude not to buy something at the stall outside the church, so I acquired some lovely silver earrings. As we trundled down bumpy one-track farm roads in our van, we saw children running barefoot with goats and fruit growing in the plantations. It felt as if we were seeing a more authentic Mexico, which was very different to the glossy, high-rise port where we were docked.

Special-interest lecturers only work on sea days as that's when passengers need a choice of entertainment. There are no duties other than delivering five different lectures. It's only since I've started travelling on my own that I've met lots of people and made friends. I make more of an effort and people make an effort with me. Richard would rather have eaten at a table for two and played on his iPad. Given the choice, now I'd always choose to work on a cruise ship rather than travel as a passenger, regardless of the financial savings. People know me because I'm introduced as a lecturer, and they feel they can talk to me. In their eyes, I'm a staff member and they often want to give me feedback about the lectures. This effect is enhanced when I run art workshops, as I have close contact with yet another group of passengers. Being an on-board entertainer means that I'm inhabiting a role and wearing an imaginary hat, which also feels empowering and gives me more confidence when interacting with strangers. With each additional cruise experience I feel my hat fits a little bit better.

I've met some other interesting lecturers along the way. One was a specialist in all things *Titanic*, which was an interesting choice for a transatlantic cruise speaker. Another was a former Hollywood journalist who'd met almost every star you could name and was able to give all the backstage gossip from years of attending the Oscars. She'd actually gone on to become good friends with some of them. For instance, she was texting her friend Nicole Kidman from the ship, updating her on our cruise adventures. We agreed that if she comes to visit Scotland she can be my guest, although I warned her that the accommodation isn't quite Hollywood standard!

Reflections on leaps of faith

I'm not someone who enjoys reading the small print, overthinks things or engages in much research or planning. I find it boring and it zaps my energy levels. But I believe this leaves me open to new opportunities, as long as they're within my physical limitations and risk tolerance. Many of my most memorable experiences and new connections have resulted from a leap of faith when I've followed my gut instincts. Giving myself permission to have fun and try new things has been key. If it doesn't work out, it just leaves me better informed for future decision making. My advice is to trust your gut.

Losing Richard was devastating and fundamentally changed my life path, but it also liberated me, affording me new opportunities that wouldn't have been possible had he still been alive. I feel a bit guilty acknowledging that feeling of liberation but it has brought such adventures. Have you experienced a similar feeling at a point of transition, for example adjusting to retirement, redundancy, bereavement or the breakdown of a relationship? Reframing these events as opportunities to move out of your comfort zone, even in tiny steps, could be the trigger you need to expand your horizons and find joy. I always seem to come back to the old saying, 'When life gives you lemons, make lemonade.'

PART 5

Going solo

CHAPTER 28

The art of solo travelling

The way in which different cruise lines manage solo travellers varies quite a bit. I'm still learning, but my observation thus far is that solo travellers probably need more support in the evenings as going for a meal in the formal dining room every night can be lonely if you're eating on your own, or sometimes hard work if you're sharing a table with different strangers every night. Introverts might avoid it altogether and order room service. If there's a pre-dinner solo traveller drinks meet-up, those who don't have plans can arrange to have dinner together and make a priority booking with the restaurant manager. Special-interest enrichment lecturers get a double room to themselves and can bring a guest if they choose to, but as I've said, I prefer not to share a cabin. I spent nearly 40 years in a happy relationship but was required to compromise, and now I've been afforded the chance to be a little selfish.

Eating breakfast and lunch alone doesn't bother me, although inevitably I meet someone I know or start chatting to the people at the adjoining table. However, eating an evening meal alone in the main restaurant when everyone else is chatting in couples or groups isn't my preferred option. Meeting solo travellers or shared dining tables avoids this option until you inevitably meet people and form friendship groups. To my surprise, the Tampa to LA Panama Canal cruise resulted in me meeting a group of friends half my age. I'd gone along to the solo traveller meet-up but there were lots of non-solo travellers there who'd just been taking part in a trivia quiz. Spotting a solo traveller among the quizzers was going to be a challenge. I noticed a young Black man with dreadlocks sitting on his own, so I got up some courage and approached him. He was indeed a solo traveller. Then two other young people joined us who were also solo travellers. Matt and Rebecca were from Canada and Ishmael from Trinidad and Tobago. After our initial meeting, I thought, that's great, they've made friends of their own age, so I'll probably never see them again. For two nights after that, I had dinner with eight strangers, who were all lovely but hard work, so I went to the evening game show on my own. It was called 'Love & Marriage', another reminder of my solo status. It was hilarious. When a 90-year-old contestant was asked to choose which description best suited what she'd see if her 93-year-old husband dropped his towel on the way out of the shower, from three options (A, Eiffel Tower; B, anaconda; or C, a Volkswagen Beetle with two burst tyres), she said, 'C – he's 93!' Not surprisingly, his answer matched. They knew each other well, were up for a laugh and won the game.

The next night, I met the thirty-somethings in the dinner queue and they invited me to join them. We had a great time and eventually made plans to eat together every night. We'd go to the theatre together after dinner and then play late-night cards while gorging on warm chocolate chip cookies. It's so nice to see young people embracing travel and forging friendships around the world. They religiously attended all my lectures, sitting in the front row. The conversation was rich and varied: politics, tattoos, homosexuality, mental health, contraception, travel, relationships, the management of dreadlocks and everything in between. As with previous cruise friendships, we exchanged addresses and hoped our paths would cross again. They've since been in touch and there may be some visitors to Scotland at some point soon. I'm amazed by how many people I've met on my solo adventures who've gone on to become friends, visitors or future travelling companions.

There are several varieties of solo travellers. I think I've met many of them during my adventures. I was in awe of a woman I met who'd been travelling around the world, mostly on land, backpacking on her own. She told me that she particularly loved Iran and Peru. You couldn't pay me enough to travel alone in a foreign country without a tour guide or group. I'd be fine making friends and talking to people, but I'd be in a constant state of heightened anxiety, and fearful of getting lost or attacked. My imagination would be on overdrive, in a negative way. However, my fellow traveller who loved backpacking in Iran struggled on a busy cruise ship and sought some solitude. Every port day, I booked an excursion so that I'd get to explore a new country safely and meet people. Every port day, she'd disembark with her backpack and stride off confidently to explore on her own. I admired her confidence and drive but have no aspiration to become a solitary explorer.

Another female solo traveller had a stuffed toy monkey with her and did a photoshoot of the toy at every port and every significant viewpoint or building so she could send photos home to her granddaughter. The monkey was 'on tour'. It was an interesting conversation starter with other guests, as she'd sometimes ask them to take a photograph of her and the monkey and, not surprisingly, like other guests, I was keen to hear the back story. What a good idea to try if you find it difficult to initiate a conversation. One thing I often do is take a photo for couples who are struggling to take a selfie. They usually start chatting as a result of the interaction. One couple even invited me to join them and bought me an ice cream as we sat in the sun near a geothermal hot spring in Japan. They told me about their difficulties in managing their son, who had schizophrenia, and I was able to offer some informal advice. They'd been attending my lectures and had found the message about not judging people with a mental illness and recognising the significant impact on families really helpful. You just never know people's stories until you make that initial connection and start chatting. With one in four people likely to be impacted by mental health problems at some point in their lives, it's likely that my message will regularly resonate with members of the audience.

There aren't many situations in which I feel awkward, but going to a formal event on my own always reminds me that Richard has gone. Inevitably, people will talk to me and I to them, but there's that brief wave of being alone that washes over me and I feel conspicuous because of my absent other half. There are two occasions that come to mind, when my butler on the five-star cruise ship came to the rescue without being prompted. The first time was when I received an invitation to the captain's drinks reception. It was a formal night, so everyone was dressed up in dinner suits and cocktail dresses. I got ready and tentatively set off for the theatre venue. En route, I passed couples and families posing for photographs and was reminded of the times when our family had done the same. These professional photographs have taken on such a cherished value, particularly now that they'll never again include Richard.

I could see a queue forming at the entrance to the theatre, where people were shaking hands with the captain and senior staff. I became aware of a row of butlers lining the corridor, dressed in their penguin suits. It reminded me of the penguin parade at the zoo when I was a child as my cute little friends wandered down the path towards me. I'd experienced the penguin parade years later, for real, in Antarctica, as they waddled down to the icy sea to dive for fish, and now here I was confronted by humans in smart tail coats and bow ties, looking like a row of penguins waiting to parade alongside me. Out stepped my butler from the line, offering his arm to escort me into the reception. I felt 'so looked after.

The next memorable moment of butler rescue came during my first cruise lecturing gig. Following one of my lectures, I was approached by a lovely couple from Belgium. The other passengers who'd queued up to ask questions were all asking about my forensic psychiatry experience and related topics, but this couple announced that they'd like to invite me to dinner at the French restaurant. I made my excuses to the solo travellers, as I wouldn't be dining with them that night, and went back to my stateroom to freshen up. While I was brushing my teeth, the doorbell rang. Who could it be? It was my smiling butler. 'Big night tonight – it's nearly time.' I had no idea what he was talking about. He obviously noted my blank expression. He continued, 'You've got your meal at 7 pm.' I didn't know how he knew I was going to dinner with the Belgians, but he obviously did. He offered his arm and escorted me to the lifts. It turned out he was my dinner hosts' butler too, and they'd told him about inviting the forensic psychiatry lecturer for dinner.

It was an interesting evening, as it turned out that my host was writing a book and keen to get my professional opinion on his plan for the worldwide management of life-sentenced prisoners being located on a desert island. So, it turned out to be more mentally taxing than just deciding whether to have profiteroles or crème brûlée for dessert. I found myself becoming quite philosophical, moralistic and an advocate for human rights. Well, that swept the cobwebs off my brain! I hope my perspective on the subject offered some objectivity and points for consideration. My request for people not to be judgemental about mentally disordered offenders obviously extended at some level to offenders without mental disorders. Leaving people on an island with no medical care and no option for rehabilitation seemed to go against basic human rights. Simple solutions are often not so simple, especially if your family is involved. There's always a context to consider.

When I left the Panama Canal cruise and flew home, I only had a six-day turnaround before flying back to Houston to join the next one, which was a transatlantic crossing. During that short window, Nadine, an author and speaker whom I'd met on the Panama Canal cruise, got in touch to check I'd got home safely. We discovered that by weird coincidence we were both going to be in Houston the following week, so we arranged to meet for dinner. That'll be another cruise buddy added to the list.

CHAPTER 29

Collecting cruise buddies

As I boarded the ship for my second lecturing gig of 2024, I was informed that the 'My Time Dining' option had been chosen for me, which meant turning up at the restaurant at 6.45 pm and being allocated a shared table with different people every night. I was ushered in to join a table of six: me; an old lady with long, white hair and one eye half shut; a couple from Texas called Grytch and Frances; a lady from Texas called Louise, who was travelling without her husband; and a widow from Australia called Miralda. The older lady complained to the waiters quite a lot and didn't seem interested in communicating with us, despite our attempts to include her. The rest of us were chatty and commenced the ritual dance of 'Who are you? Where are you from? What do you do? Have you cruised before?' We got on well. The waiter noted the camaraderie and at the end of the first meal said that, if we wanted, we could opt to book the table for future evenings and stay together. Collective nods sealed the deal. The older lady opted not to return to our table two nights in, but continued to give us the evil eye each time we entered the restaurant. The poor soul may have had facial palsy, but her dismissive and unfriendly manner meant she still got the 'stink eye' label from my dinner companions.

We continued to build our new friendships. My dinner mates became regular attendees at my lectures, sitting at the front of the theatre, waving and clapping. After the second lecture, they hung around and invited me for lunch. We ate many lunches and evening meals together after that. The other ladies enjoyed a flutter in the casino. That's not for me, but I'd watch them play for a while and cheer them on. Frances believed that rubbing her chest on the slot machine made it lucky, so there was some giggly cavorting and winning of $2 every so often. It wasn't necessarily high-roller material, but a laugh all the same. The other two ladies were more committed to the cause and both won enough points in the casino for a 'free' cruise. I suspect that you had to spend quite a lot in the casino to 'win' a free cruise! More often than not, I'd watch for 20 minutes then head off to watch the theatre show.

One night, Frances, Grytch and I sat talking for so long after dinner that we missed the casino and the show altogether. Then we heard an announcement that the restaurant would be closing in five minutes. We looked around, and the several hundred other passengers who'd been in the restaurant had all left. We sheepishly apologised to the staff and departed, still chatting as we walked along the ship's promenade. We stopped off at the cafe for a slice of pizza and freshly made chocolate chip cookies, which was fatal for my ongoing diet efforts. We'd only just finished a three-course meal! As the cruise progressed, our friendship grew.

Frances: 'Are you coming back to Galveston for your Caribbean cruise in November?'

Me: 'Yes.'

Frances: 'We'll pick you up at the airport, you can stay at our house in Houston and we'll take you to the port in the morning. We're thinking we might book the cruise and come with you too.'

Louise: 'I might ask my husband if he fancies a Caribbean cruise and we could maybe come as well.'

I guess that's another three people added to my cruise buddy list. Some people collect stamps, coins, toy cars or paintings, but I seemed to be collecting Texan cruise buddies. What is it about Texans and cruising? I met my first Texan cruisers, Karen, Jimmy, Gail and Richard, on the New Zealand cruise trivia team, and now we've become friends to visit and travel with. I met my next Texans on the Galveston to Barcelona cruise. I've already visited them and we've travelled together to the Caribbean.

There's a relaxed, friendly disposition and a genuine interest in people that radiates from all of them, which makes for easy conversation and companionship. What I've found is that if I'm open to making friends, friends will find me and seem to stick with me. My previous career and personal story seem to be of some interest, which may be an initial hook, but being open, friendly and chatty does the rest – and I can chat! I also think that natural storytellers tend to attract each other. It's easy to engage with people who give interesting accounts of their adventures or are articulate and humorous when talking about their everyday experiences. It's their use of language and how they perceive the world that's interesting to me as it shows how their mind works. It's most interesting when their take on a situation is quirky or slightly at odds with my own. I don't like negativity, though.

Not everyone collects cruise buddies, but it's humbling to know some people have collected several examples of my artwork instead, including paintings, prints, merchandise, cards and glasswork. It seems that Rhona Morrison Art, despite being inexpensive, has become a tiny bit collectable. When Fraser and Jill moved into their new homes, they both requested some of my artwork for their houses. That was the highest endorsement for my work, not just as an artist, but as a mum. Fraser and Alisa moved house again recently and requested five more pictures.

When people collect things, often the age of the item affects its worth. Not so with cruise buddies! My youngest friends are in their twenties and the oldest over 80. Age is just a number and I'm sticking to that, especially as mine advances. Each person has their own unique value and we need to celebrate that. After all, within the rich tapestry of life, you hear of octogenarians running marathons for charity and young footballers campaigning for free school meals. You can't compare. The person behind the individual stories is what's important. But you do meet an interesting bunch of people on cruise ships. It's only when you sit down with someone for a couple of hours that you really find out what makes them tick. I was having such a chat with a lovely man who'd been widowed the year before. His wife died of presenile dementia and he'd been her carer. It seemed that he'd started to grieve before she died, just as I did with Richard, as we'd both been in the position of losing a little bit of the person we loved, a day at a time, right until the end. Our conversation took a turn when we talked about what we'd done since. I talked about writing my memoir and, as with many other people I've spoken to, he told me that his friends had told him he should write a book about his life. It was only then that he disclosed that he was a trained alligator hunter! One day, he found a large alligator in the middle of the road. Upon calling the local authorities, he was given permission to intervene. It was an unplanned event, so he didn't follow the normal procedure, which was to tire the animal out first. He threw a sheet over its head, got it between his legs and started to wrestle with it. He decided to roll it towards the softer grass verge but the alligator grabbed his groin in its teeth, before struggling to get away again. After the incident, he saw blood pouring down his legs from the teeth marks on both his thighs and groin. A trip to the hospital was inevitable. When he arrived at the ER, he was informed he'd need to take a seat as there would be quite a delay. He told the nurse that he couldn't sit down because 'An alligator bit my balls!' He was then rushed into a side room to wait for a doctor. He slipped off his shorts to reveal bleeding thighs and testicles now the size of tennis balls. The receptionist nearly collapsed at the sight when she re-entered the room to ask a follow-up question. Now, an alligator bite to the groin is certainly up there with the most book-worthy stories I've heard!

The excursions on this trip were limited in number but not in quality. I particularly enjoyed my day in the Azores at the crater lake and glorious botanical gardens, the caves of Nerja in Malaga with their stalactites and stalagmites, and my walking tour of Valencia's stunning old town. I'm always left with a taste of the place and a desire to see more.

Collecting cruise buddies from all around the globe has been fun, but it becomes even better when I start bumping into them again on my travels or they've made a special effort to visit me in Scotland. Each connection began with a simple, polite conversation in a queue, at a dinner table, travelling in an elevator or at a solo traveller meet-up. It's a bit like planting a seed in the garden – sometimes a small plant will appear and, if nurtured, it will grow. Relationships are just like that – they spring up in unlikely situations and only a select few survive, as long as you pay attention to them.

Many seasoned travellers are loyal to one particular cruise line as over time they spend sufficient nights at sea to rack up loyalty points and get free drinks, complimentary Wi-Fi, free laundry, pre-dinner canapés, cocktail receptions with the captain and sometimes a free cruise. Inevitably, even after only two years of lecturing on different ships, I've already started bumping into people with whom I've cruised before, having met them at dinner, in trivia teams, on excursions or at meet-ups, and some who have previously attended my lectures. It's truly humbling to know that some of these passengers have read my book and even gone on to book a cruise knowing that I'll be on it. These travellers have become friends. Cruise buddies from Toronto, Texas and New York have visited me in Scotland and

I've been to visit my friends in Texas. I'm hopeful that friends from Canada, Trinidad and Tobago, Australia and Texas will visit soon and I hope to catch up with another globetrotting friend from Newfoundland when I cruise there in the summer of 2025, if she's not off travelling again! It's such a privilege being part of a truly international network of globetrotters. I never dreamed that my book would open so many doors in retirement. Being open to trying new things has brought such rewards.

Chapter 30

I'm free...

Later that year, I took three further cruises. The first was with a group of 20 fellow Rotarians, as we celebrated our club's 50th anniversary with a two-week Mediterranean cruise. This was quite a departure for me because for the past six years I've travelled on my own. My friend Elaine and her husband Brian were particularly considerate, offering transport to and from the port in Southampton. They also included me in their bookings for theatre shows and speciality dining. It was a huge success, but travelling with several married couples inevitably highlighted Richard's absence and my single status, even though I was never excluded or treated differently. There's still that uneven number at the table and the empty seat reminder. I chose to book my excursions separately from everyone else, to give some time just for me, as I've learned that I enjoy the freedom of meeting random people in tour groups. I must admit that, despite the good company of my friends, I missed attending the solo traveller meet-ups. I managed to get along to a couple but was never in a position to join any group activities as I already had plans with my Rotary pals. I enjoyed cheesemaking in Cadiz; a train ride tour of Tarragona; visits to quaint hilltop villages in Provence; a trip on a vintage train to Soller, near Palma; and a tapas walking trail in La Coruña. The rain in La Spezia didn't dampen our spirits as we sat under a canopy and enjoyed each other's company. The food, company and the live entertainment were excellent, so the evenings were always particularly enjoyable.

A matter of a few weeks later, I was off lecturing again, on a transpacific cruise from Seattle to Tokyo, which was essentially ten sea days and four ports in Japan. I was a bit apprehensive about the extended period at sea and how I'd fill my time in between lectures, but I shouldn't have worried. I met the biggest, friendliest group of solo travellers yet. There was a fairly even gender split, a wide age range, and we were from truly international backgrounds: Australia, the Netherlands, the US, the UK, Mexico and Chile. We had pre- and post-dinner meet-ups, pizza breaks, games of bingo, theatre trips, speciality dining and some even attended my lectures. A Rotarian called Justin, from Arkansas, gave me a pennant for my club. We were from such diverse backgrounds that dinner conversations were always entertaining. One male passenger surprised me by telling me he'd previously been imprisoned for hacking into the NASA computer system and had packed a drone in his case, along with a top hat! We even found ourselves discussing upside-down pineapple magnets on stateroom doors, which apparently signal 'swingers' are welcome. Who knew?! I used to like eating pineapples, but now they have a whole new connotation. I found myself looking differently at men wearing Hawaiian shirts featuring pineapples. Was that just a coincidence or was there some hidden message? I wasn't about to ask! Did someone mention Trump? That was a hot pre-election topic, to be avoided on a ship full of Americans.

Previously, my lectures had been delivered on stage in a traditional theatre setting. Here, I was in an unusual setting with a huge, three-storey glass wall curving around behind me, so I had a backdrop of a vast expanse of sea and sky with my PowerPoint on a screen to the side. The seats were on different levels and in odd configurations around the room, so it was slightly disconcerting looking out at the audience, but I coped. People were still queuing up after the lectures to have a chat and one lady surprised me by telling me that she believed she'd had a close encounter, near-miss experience with the notorious serial killer Ted Bundy when she was at university. As you can imagine, that made for an unexpected and fascinating post-lecture chat.

The professional entertainment on board was great, although I didn't opt for the simulated skydiving, surfing, bumper cars or laser tag, as I'm quite happy to see the shows and read a book. I did the simulated skydiving years ago during a family holiday and loved it, but I probably exceed the weight limit now! I booked excursions to a bear ranch, the lake, a viewpoint, a lighthouse, a folkloric museum, a temple, a tea ceremony and a Mount Fuji viewpoint. I even made a block print of a Japanese scene at the museum.

However, my most memorable excursion of that trip was revisiting Hakodate. I'd been there 18 months earlier at cherry blossom time, so I thought a further visit to the stunning, star-shaped park in autumn would be worthwhile. I'd teamed up with a lovely couple from Seattle, whom I met in the queue for the excursion bus. We'd been given some free time in the park, so we wandered around taking photos, as tourists do. We came upon a little Japanese man with a stall who was hiring out kimonos and samurai outfits by the hour for photoshoots. As a nation, the Japanese are noted for their polite, respectful behaviour. I could almost see the cogs in his head turning as he debated how to tell this big Scottish woman that his petite kimono was unlikely to fit. It may have gone around one leg, but certainly not two legs, a bum and a stomach! My new friend Beth from Seattle read my mind. She held up one kimono back to front and I stuck my hands in the sleeves. Now that my stomach was covered with cerise floral silk, I could slip the next matching kimono on like a coat that wouldn't do up. Phew! The Japanese man sprang into action and sorted me out with a sash, cord, bustle, hairpin, parasol, fan and bag. Time for a photoshoot!

As my friends proceeded to get dressed in their outfits, I became a little distracted by a Japanese gentleman in an orange hat who was standing a short distance away. He had nothing to do with our tour group, but I thought, 'I know that man, that's Roy!'

Eighteen months earlier, during my first lecturing gig, I'd been allowed to act as a tour escort to support the local guide on an excursion. As it was my first time, I had a photograph taken in front of the bus with the tour guide, a quirky little man called Roy. He possessed the rare skill of being able to have a sense of humour in a second language. It was definitely him, so I quickly scrolled through my phone and found the photo. All he saw as I strolled over to him was a big, blonde woman in a kimono, balancing a parasol, a fan, a bag, a bright yellow backpack and a mobile phone. When I opened my mouth, he then had to cope with the Scottish accent. 'Hello, we met last year,' I said, as I thrust the photo under his nose. 'That's never happened before,' he said. 'Can I take a photo of your photo?' I wonder what he said when he got home? 'I took a selfie with a big, blonde, Scottish woman in a kimono today.' I love chance encounters like that.

Back on the ship, when I was talking about my early life and what influenced my career choice, I mentioned that I was born in a castle. Well, Lennox Castle Hospital, to be precise. After the lecture, a man came up to the side of the stage and said, 'Guess where I was born?' You guessed it, it was Lennox Castle. The more I travel, the more I realise what a small world it is.

One night towards the end of the cruise, I spotted an email on my phone from my agent in Florida, asking if I could stay on board for a further two weeks because the next lecturer had cancelled. Did I want to travel to ports in Japan, South Korea, Taiwan, Vietnam, Hong Kong and Singapore? Well, that was an easy reply, but only after I'd checked in back home, to make sure Mum didn't miss out on visits. I'd be saying goodbye to my new friends Melody, Anders, Justin and crew in Tokyo, but Nora was staying on. We befriended some Australian ladies on the next leg of the cruise, as well as Craig, who was working on the ship to upgrade the IT system. We chatted every evening and became friends. I'd be making full use of laundry services on this next leg of the trip as I had no clean clothes left! It was agreed that I could run some art classes. I was surprised to find a three-year-old and her father in the group. She managed to produce a perfect pointillism egg drawing, keeping her dots inside the lines and even managing the graded shading. Amazing!

There were a lot more ports this time, so there was plenty to see and do. I went on to visit samurai castles and beautiful temples and shrines; took a trip on a gigantic big wheel with a complete stranger I met in the queue as were getting off the tour bus; visited a historic village museum and volcanic crater in Jeju Island, South Korea; sailed in a sampan in Hong Kong's Aberdeen Harbour among a floating village of boats; went to the Peak viewpoint for a bird's eye view over Hong Kong; went to a cookery school in Vietnam, where we made a delicious meal and visited the stunning Orchid Garden; and the Merlion fountain in Singapore, before finally heading home. It did cross my mind that if the publishing of my book in Taiwan had been more advanced, I could've organised a book launch while I was there, but it wasn't to be. It would've been pretty cool, though.

I'd been at sea for a month. The demographics of the passengers on this cruise were noticeably different from many other cruises, with a high proportion of Asians. The entertainment on offer had to take account of that. When daily stretch and Zumba sessions were going on, they needed a huge venue to accommodate literally hundreds of Asians of all ages who flocked to the venue for every session. I'd been aware of the cultural interest in tai chi and related practices when I'd visited China and Japan previously, but it was really highlighted on this ship. There were also a lot of Americans on the trans-atlantic crossing, so one of the speakers, who talked about a popular American TV actor, always drew a good crowd. I suspect he's less likely to get booked as a speaker for a Medi-terranean cruise, though. Fortunately, my topic has a more general appeal, regardless of the audience.

CHAPTER 31

Two sex bombs, anyone?

Back home, I had two weeks to wash my clothes and visit friends and family before I was off again for my Caribbean lecturing gig with my Texan buddies. I seemed to be flying across the Atlantic and Pacific oceans more often than I drove my car into Glasgow or prepared myself a home-cooked meal. It was becoming a bit of a surreal blur, albeit a very enjoyable one.

As planned, when I arrived in Houston, Frances and Grytch generously hosted me. Once on board ship in the Caribbean, I enjoyed the hospitality and company of my four Texan friends every evening for dinner but went on excursions at ports on my own as I'd never visited Cozumel in Mexico, Grand Cayman, Curaçao or Aruba. There were lots of beautiful beaches, with crystal-clear water lapping up onto palm tree-lined sandy coves against backdrops of brightly painted buildings. But, true to form, I'd booked some more adventurous excursions to see caves with stalactites and stalagmites; a trip underwater in a semi-submersible submarine to see a shipwreck surrounded by lots of vibrant tropical fish; a visit to a place called Hell, so that I could say 'I've been to Hell and back'; and a visit to ruined Mayan temples where I ended up with two parrots and a monkey on my shoulders.

One evening, as I reached the entrance to the theatre, I was stopped by the activities manager, Bern, who was greeting guests who'd come to see the Tom Jones tribute act. He asked if I could do him a favour. Naturally, as he was one of my bosses on board, I said yes. He reached into a carrier bag and produced a pair of bright orange lacy panties, which quite frankly wouldn't have fitted around one of my legs. Somewhat aghast, I awaited my instructions. Apparently, I'd need to launch them on stage when the performer (Daniel, the cruise director) was cavorting around the stage, thrusting his pelvis in my direction, to the song 'Sex Bomb'. This would mean sitting in the front row. As the show progressed, I felt more and more uneasy, worried that I was the only one with lacy panties secreted in my handbag. What a relief when two other ladies in the front row stood up with me and launched their lace. Phew! I told my friends back home and they asked, 'Did anyone see that it was you?' Only the whole auditorium!

Having slinked out of the theatre feeling just a little embarrassed, I thought that was the end of it, but no. The next morning, at the breakfast buffet, I was loading my bowl with crunchy granola when I was approached by a five-year-old boy who said, 'I see you at the theatre every night.' I asked him if he'd been enjoying all the shows. 'Yes. I saw you throwing something onto the stage.' I could feel a pink flush appearing on my cheeks. 'In my defence, they made me do it!' There wasn't much more to say, really. Fame at last...

I always try to sit near the front in a theatre because I like to see the whites of the performer's eyes. However, since taking to the stage for my cruise lecturing, I have an added reason for sitting near the front. As a performer, I now understand the benefit of having the audience in my sightline to engage and interact with. So, with that in mind, there I was in the front row for the Elvis tribute act. He looked like Elvis, sounded like Elvis, and the orchestra was fabulous. He was a few numbers in when, uh-oh, what was happening? He headed for the stairs and out into the audience, hips thrusting, fingers running through his black quiff. He ended up in front of me and I seemed to be having a lap dance from Elvis! His piercing blue eyes were about six inches from mine and he was looking into my soul as he serenaded me. There was nowhere to look. That familiar flush returned. Who'd have thought I'd have encounters with Tom Jones and Elvis in the same week? Feeling a bit hot and sweaty had nothing to do with the Caribbean sun!

So far, I've been collecting cruise buddies in New Zealand, the Far East, Japan, on transatlantic crossings and now in the Caribbean, and my adventure with Texans Frances, Grytch, Louise and John was no different. It resulted in some new additions, including 'Pete and Repeat'. Well, Pete's wife was actually called Becky, but she informed us that his previous partner was also called Becky, so it's easier to remember! We got to spend quite a bit of time together, as we picked similar excursions. They also came to my lectures and art classes, and we went for lunch and played cards. They'd set their alarm in time to make it to the 9 am lectures and then went for breakfast afterwards. Several people reported setting their alarms to ensure they didn't miss my lectures, which was really lovely, especially as they were supposed to be relaxing on holiday.

Occasionally, strangers would approach me around the ship and share stories related to mental illness. On one such occasion, a passenger disclosed having worked with some 'interesting' psychiatry colleagues, including someone who played cello naked in their garden and another who used a chainsaw to cut an additional exit in their office wall as they didn't want the inconvenience of having to walk round the long way! I thought I had some odd colleagues, but not as extreme as that.

It was interesting to hear from my new Texan friends that the individual states in the US are a bit like independent countries, with different laws and mentalities. It appears that the friendly Texan mentality aligns with my own, so perhaps I could be an honorary Texan. I certainly have enough invitations to visit and go on future holidays with them. When I was working as a forensic psychiatrist and associate medical director and had to complete a personality profile, I also became more aware of the characteristics I'm more attracted to in others. I don't think 'Texan' was one of the options in the test, although as I was scored as an ENTP on the Myers–Briggs scale, perhaps the 'T' actually stands for Texan after all!

I'm lucky enough to have travelled extensively over the past 20 years and visited places such as China, Russia, Dubai, Alaska, Antarctica, Canada, the US and Europe, but I wonder what next year's cruises will bring? With trips already planned on a new cruise line that include ports in Iceland, Greenland, Newfoundland and Morocco, which I've never visited, I can't wait. I'm having the ride of my life, but it all started by taking a leap of faith and joining this network of globetrotters on this roller coaster of opportunity, and just strapping myself in.

During my travels, I've also met many over-55s from the US and Australia, who've told me that they've moved into retirement communities. This concept feels unfamiliar and a bit unusual for Scotland. However, one lady from Arizona described her community by saying, 'It's like kindergarten for adults – we just play all day.' She went on to describe playing cards over a glass of wine, going for a swim, dance classes, her friend hosting a Thanksgiving dinner, a group going off on a cruise together, gardening, the bridge club and blossoming friendships. It sounded like a younger version of the retirees in Richard Osman's 2020 book, *The Thursday Murder Club*, which is set in a retirement village where a group of retirees get up to all sorts of mischief. I guess I thought that if I got to the stage of giving up my home and moving to a retirement village, I'd be on a slippery slope towards old age and my final years. But these retirees seemed to see it as a licence to party with their pals next door. Some of these partygoers were travelling in small groups but others on their own, with their friends back home watching their houses and watering the plants. What shone through was that they all felt part of a truly integrated, supportive and vibrant community, and felt they had permission to live it up a bit. These were positive life moves at an age when they could enjoy the freedom and sense of community that their new location afforded them. The cheeky 'kindergarten for adults' description felt joyous.

Talking of *The Thursday Murder Club*, as a forensic psychiatrist I had to interview hundreds of murderers during my career. Many of the offenders I saw had a history of violence, including murder, rape and also stalking. Since retirement, I'm pleased to say that I haven't had to deal with the same clientele, although I have had to listen to passengers 'murder' a song during a karaoke competition and watch passengers 'indecently expose' themselves at the swimming pool. I've still only had one stalker, but I do have cruise buddies who seem to be following me around the globe, and I like that. Karen, Jimmy, Nancy and Irene followed me to Antarctica; Liz, Vihan, Nancy, Irene, Karen, Jimmy, Gail and Richard followed me to Scotland; and Frances, Grytch and Louise followed me to the Caribbean. I must confess that I started the trend by travelling to Texas to see Karen and Jimmy, so I'm guilty as charged.

CHAPTER 32

Leaving a positive legacy

W hen I started enrichment lecturing, I had no idea what size of audience to expect. My fear was that absolutely no one would turn up. Although still relatively new to the profession, I've now completed seven cruises as a lecturer on a variety of ships, on different routes, at different levels of luxury and with passengers who fit different demographics. During this time, I've had the opportunity to observe attendance patterns for both the special-interest lectures and paid professional entertainers. Obviously, it helps if you're good, but timing is everything on a cruise ship. What time is your slot in relation to dining room serving patterns? How close is it to clashing with breakfast, lunch or dinner, as food is always a priority for passengers, despite 24-hour access to food on board? Was yesterday a sea day, when they may have stayed up late for a few tipples or a flutter in the casino? Was there a time change moving the clock forward during the night? Does it clash with sunbathing by the pool? Bridge lessons? A dance class? Daytime trivia? Once you realise this, you can almost predict the attendance and overcome the fear of not being good enough.

There were lots of sea days on my transatlantic cruise, with multiple time changes overnight and some 9.30 am lecture slots. Not surprisingly, my 10.30 am slot was busier. A long lie-in and breakfast were likely to have taken priority. The lady from the cruise line who was supporting the lecturers came along to my first couple of lectures to make sure that the tech was OK and to rate the quality of the presentations. These were probably my busiest as they were mid-morning lectures. She counted more than 400 people in the audience each time, by far the biggest audience I'd lectured to on a cruise ship thus far. The three-tier theatre was very grand and had a capacity of 1,200. Fortunately, at the end of the cruise, I received a five-star rating, so I was delighted. My early morning slots weren't quite as busy, but I had a very loyal following who came to all the lectures, not just my new cruise mates from my dinner table.

It was important to overcome my self-attached 'technophobe' label to understand how to connect my laptop to each ship's equipment and to work out how to use the head mic or handheld mic, if offered. I'm certainly learning about technology, so that's a bit of personal development right there. It'll be interesting to review my royalty statements to see if lecturing on these bigger ships is reflected in book sales. With the data always several months out of date, it may be difficult to establish a correlation. What's clear, though, is that my message is getting out to a much wider international audience and that's good either way. I feel grateful every time a passenger approaches me to tell me that the content had meaning for them.

I think we all hope to leave a positive legacy, whether it be within our family, friendships or workplace. When I embarked on my post-retirement adventures, writing my memoir, lecturing on cruise ships and producing artwork, I guess I hadn't really stopped to consider the impact that I might have, having stumbled into all of it without a lot of pre-planning. However, as I've said before, if only one person in a lecture theatre, one reader of my book or one person in my art class takes something positive from my input, that's good enough. Not everyone has to love what I do. I've been humbled by the number of people who have come to talk to me after lectures, shared personal stories, taken something from the art classes or reviewed my book so positively. The messages and lessons will be different for everyone, within their own personal context. The messages in my first memoir are simple and I make no apology for repeating them here. Sometimes mental illness makes good people do bad things. It was my job to find them, treat them and rehabilitate them. Every mentally disordered offender is someone's child and didn't ask to be ill. How would you want your child to be treated? Try to see the human beings behind the newspaper headlines. Ask people what matters to them. If one of my chats with a business owner helps them achieve their goal, if a charity is able to have more impact because of my fundraising via Rotary or if recording my audiobook helps someone with visual impairment access my book, then it's been worth it.

During one of my art workshops, I wandered around each table to find out how people were finding the pointillism exercise I'd given them and sharing tips on technique. I came to a table where a passenger wearing a hat was so hunched over their piece of paper that I couldn't determine if they were young, old, male or female. 'How are you enjoying the exercise?' No response. 'I see you're trying the koi carp. Are you going to give it a name?' No response. The lady next to the person in the hat looked over and said, 'Why don't you call it Dorothy?' Still no response. I moved on to talk to people at the other side of the table, but felt bad about my inability to engage with the passenger in the hat. At the end of the 90-minute class, the lady beside the person in the hat approached me. 'Thank you so much. My daughter has cerebral palsy. She managed to sit for the whole session. Look at what she did.' She then produced a pointillism picture of an egg, which had been the starter exercise to practise the technique.

'Look at that. She kept all the dots inside the egg and even managed to follow the shading you suggested. I can't believe it.'

'Do you think she enjoyed it?'

'Yes, look at her koi carp.'

She had doodled a bit around the outside, but she'd still attempted the shading with dots on the fish.

'I guess it has helped her concentration and manual dexterity. Would you like some more blank templates for her? You can keep the pen.'

'Thank you so much. Yes, she'd love that.'

There may have been 45 passengers in the class, but it was that one silent girl in the hat who made it all worthwhile.

Not everyone will do something that makes headline news, but we can all aspire to be a pebble in a pool, causing ripples around us that touch others in a positive way. When I delivered my pointillism art workshop during my Caribbean cruise adventure, my aim was simply to entertain the passengers, but one mother spoke to me afterwards and told me she has three neurodivergent family members and they'd all found the pointillism workshop incredibly calming. The following day, her teenage daughter came up to me after the session, gave me a hug and said, 'I really liked that. I tend to have a really busy head and get overstimulated, but this helped me stay calm. I'm going to do this when I get home.' That experience made it all worthwhile. To have caused that ripple effect for that family surprised me and made me smile. These small, unexpected experiences feed my soul.

Reflections on going solo

My main reflection is that cruising is a safe and enjoyable way for a solo traveller to see the world (but definitely not during the school holidays!). You get to choose how much or how little you wish to engage with others, depending on your personal preferences. I've met so many lovely people at solo traveller meet-ups and on excursions that I now have a network of contacts across the world.

However, solo travelling doesn't need to involve holidays. It can just be about journeying through life as a single person, however you've arrived at that situation. My impression remains the same, in that single people can have just as much fun and feel just as fulfilled as those in relationships, sometimes even more so, due to the feeling of liberation and fewer constraints. A factor that I believe affects how fulfilled people feel is their willingness to be open to new opportunities and then embrace them. What individuals feel comfortable with varies enormously, as that's what makes human beings so unique, so we each need to walk our own path. I might be willing to stand on stage and talk to 400 strangers, whereas others will find it a challenge to make small talk to a stranger sitting next to them at the theatre. Both activities could take you into your stretch and growth area.

It's back to that old saying, 'horses for courses'. If you feel relaxed and happy, you're more likely to enjoy the experience. Getting to know your own happy, relaxed place is key, although challenging yourself a little is always good, within limits.

PART 6

From baby boomer to late bloomer

CHAPTER 33

Flower of Scotland

'm not much of a gardener. Well, that's not true. That implies I dabble, when in fact I pay someone to cut and treat my lawn (which is mostly moss, due to clay soil and poor drainage), and that's about it! However, have you noticed that some people start to bloom in retirement? They somehow seem brighter and fresher. At work, I wore mostly what I thought were business-appropriate colours – black, navy and grey – but, as I approached retirement, some colour started to creep in. Six years on and I'm a bit of a kaleidoscope. My hair is lighter, with the help of my amazing hairdresser, Derek. My clothes are now lime green, orange, cerise, bright blue and yellow, often all at the same time, with matching shoes and jewellery. It just makes me feel happy. I definitely think that work, and what we often assume people will expect or think, can constrain our personal growth. When pressure and expectations are parked to the side, we bloom. Well, that's been my experience, anyway. I now feel more like a flower of Scotland than I was ten years ago, despite the age-o-meter having kicked on a bit. Just like nurturing a garden, I've been tending to myself a bit more, thinking more seriously about skincare, fitness and weight. I know I should eat more fruit, veg, fibre and protein and reduce carbs, but I hardly ever shop for food or cook as this retiree is a lady who lunches – a lot. Garden centre caramel shortcake is my kryptonite. I seem to lose all willpower when it's within about ten metres. So, I do think more about weight and diet; I just haven't mastered the addressing it bit! Six cruises this year didn't help the dieting cause either.

In 2024, part of our Rotary Club's 50th-birthday celebration included planting 50 fruit trees in the local community, split into mini orchards around the town. I tend to support most of our activities, but I've been noticeably absent from a lot of the environmental projects as it's not really my forte. I've helped with litter picking, but my involvement in planting purple crocuses to raise awareness of our End Polio Now campaign was restricted to encouraging the children from our Rotakids Club to plant them in the school grounds and explaining the rationale for this. I have dodgy knees, which makes kneeling down almost impossible as it's excruciatingly painful and I struggle to get back up. However, I went along to one of the tree-planting sessions. Truth be told, I managed to dig half a hole to plant one tree, but hit a boulder and a block of wood and needed some assistance from some of the stronger Rotarians. However, I did manage the less physically challenging job of ferrying trees from the car and cutting the netting to form a protective barrier from hungry deer. I'm more useful wrapping up the hamper prize for our silent disco fundraiser or providing some home baking for my turn on the rota to support Andy's Man Club, which is a vital local resource supporting men with mental health challenges. As a club we are quite unusual. Historically, Rotary Clubs consisted of male, often retired businessmen. Rotary is now technically open to men and women, with a wide age range. However, several clubs continue to have a mostly ageing membership of men. Not in Kilsyth Rotary! We have an age range of 30 to 80 and more women than men in our club, so within that we bring diverse types of energy, ideas, skills and experience. In days gone by, I don't think silent discos and murder mystery dinners would've featured in the social calendar.

Another community that bloomed was a splinter group of Scottish authors who emerged from the Write That Book Facebook group. Initially, the meetings were held in the private room of Bertie's Proper Fish & Chips in Edinburgh. It was at one of these meetings that I tried my first deep-fried Mars Bar (for readers outside the UK, this is a bar of yummy chocolate and soft toffee, which was never designed to be covered in batter or deep fried). As it gets a mention in my memoir, it was only right that I should sample it a few times at subsequent meetings, with ice cream (very sweet and calorie laden). Although we met in a private side room, the entrance was open to the main restaurant, so it could get a little noisy. As an alternative, we arranged for afternoon tea at my house. Fortunately, my author friend Debra, who used to own a cafe, leapt into action, making multiple cakes and scones and individual pots of homemade jam. She also brought individual three-tier cake stands for everyone. It all looked very professional. The cakes even had miniature fondant books sitting on top of them with 'WTB' on the cover! I volunteered to tackle the savouries.

During these mutually supportive catch-ups, we shared our progress and learned from each other's journeys and experience. Several of us have now been published, which is great. Some are on to their second, third and fourth books, in all sorts of genres. Some authors have even travelled down from the Highlands of Scotland for these meetings, which shows a significant degree of engagement, friendship and support. The process of writing and publishing a book involves significant self-doubt and imposter syndrome, fluctuating motivation and general angst, so someone having your back who can empathise, sympathise and encourage you is highly necessary. The unboxing of the first copies is a bit of a surreal moment. All that blood, sweat and tears wrapped up in a glossy paperback book with your name on it gives you an overwhelming feeling of 'I did it'. The feel and the weight of the first book in your hand when you lift it from the box is hard to describe. My subsequent discussion with the publisher a few months later, to give the go-ahead to a second print run because the first thousand paperbacks had sold out, was something of a milestone for me. I wasn't doing this to make my money back; I just wanted to do some good. I'm fortunate that I can afford to back myself. But the book was actually selling. Wow! I was a blossoming author, too.

The unexpected opportunities kept on coming. I usually delete emails from unknown sources without reading them, but the one from Jordan, the editor of *Art Etcetera*, caught my eye. He'd contacted me to ask if I'd like to be featured in a six-page special in his magazine. Who's going to turn that down? We had a lovely long Zoom call, after which he said he'd write a six-page article about my pen-and-ink pointillism, accompanied by photos of my favourite examples. His magazines are themed, so this would be in the 'ink' edition. He has an interest in history, so always includes a bit of historical material in relation to each topic. I made sure to include my drawing of a tiger cub as that was how Jordan first found me. I didn't know if it would generate any work for my art business, but it was a privilege to be singled out for having expertise in that area. It shows the importance of having a website and social media presence. Sometime later, I was also able to donate a print of an otter to the Otter Trust charity art auction. They'd seen a pointillism image of an otter on my website. Using my art to help with fundraising is an easy way to give back to the community.

After dogs, wedding venues have become the most popular request for my art commissions. Increasingly, couples have all the household appliances, glasses and crockery they require, so buying wedding gifts can be challenging. People often turn to me for an affordable, personal gift that you won't find on the high street – a painting of the wedding venue, often with the bride and groom's names and the date of their nuptials on the mount. I've painted several popular Scottish venues, as well as produced a pen-and-ink pointillism drawing featuring Charles Rennie Mackintosh's famous House for an Art Lover building in Glasgow for my nephew Gavin's wedding. However, I have one particular claim to fame. I was asked to paint a church in England for my tennis partner Marissa's relative. It turns out that the bride and groom are quite famous. The bride is Elon Musk's ex-wife Tallulah Riley, an accomplished actress. Her groom is also an actor, Thomas Brody-Sangster, whom I remember best as a child actor. He played a lovesick teenage drummer in the movie *Love, Actually*. The church is pretty special to the couple, so I hope they liked it.

Some other slightly unusual commission requests have included a hamster, a lion and a goat on top of a mountain, a rainbow fairy and two guinea pigs. The pet portrait requests are predominantly for dogs, several of which are now dead. When I tell my family 'I'm off to paint a dead dog', they just roll their eyes. I was once asked to paint a cat as a wedding present when the cat didn't even belong to the bride and groom. Apparently, it used their house like a second home, so they felt as if it was theirs. If the owners couldn't find their cat, they'd call their neighbours to locate it, so they thought they might like a painting of Gizmo to keep. The paintings proved to be particularly popular during the pandemic when the shops were closed and people were stuck at home. They'd simply send me a photo, I'd paint it and then post it off in special packaging, which protected the frame and glass. I've successfully shipped paintings to the US and Canada without incident. My Auntie Chris in New York even ordered a pet portrait for her very supportive neighbours. When the parcel arrived in New York, she asked her neighbour to open the fragile parcel for her as her vision was poor and she feared damaging what was inside. Imagine his surprise when he opened up the parcel to reveal a painting of his dog!

Another special painting involved a rose bush. It was special for several reasons. I had managed to contact an old school friend called Stuart via LinkedIn. We first met aged five at primary school and knew each other until we left school in 1980. He noticed that I'd started an art business and got in touch to request a painting for an elderly uncle whose wife had died. The old man had planted a standard rose bush in the garden, in her memory, so I was asked to paint a garden with a rose bush in the centre for his birthday. When it was ready, I contacted Stuart to arrange delivery. He agreed to pop over to collect it, as he was procurator fiscal on a fatal accident inquiry nearby. As he came striding down the path, it was as if there hadn't been a 40-year gap in contact. What a great night we had reminiscing. A friendship was rekindled right there, over a rose bush and a pepperoni pizza. Stuart and his wife Annie are now good friends and we catch up regularly for food, cruise chat and theatre trips.

Stuart went on to introduce me to his friend Willie, a senior lecturer in criminology at Abertay University. They knew each other from police days, when Stuart was in the fraud squad at Scotland Yard and his friend worked with the gangs in Glasgow. I went on to have the pleasure of lecturing to the criminology students – just another fortuitous contact and opportunity to spread the message in my book and challenge mindsets around the issue of mentally disordered offenders.

CHAPTER 34

Mum the legend

As a forensic psychiatrist, my mission in life was to find, treat and rehabilitate mentally disordered offenders. Their illness and offence didn't define them, but they'd need to respect and learn from the situation they found themselves in and take actions to reduce future risk of illness relapse and offending. There are parallels with other disorders unrelated to mental illness. It's important to diagnose diabetes and treat it. If the patient doesn't respect their illness, follow the correct diet and take medication or go for regular eye checks and chiropody appointments, they risk a multitude of problems, including blindness, leg ulcers, amputations and potential collapse into coma. The attitude of the general public towards a diagnosis of schizophrenia versus diabetes is often very different, with more tolerance shown towards the person with diabetes, despite schizophrenia being genetically inherited, outside the person's control and the diabetes in some cases being related to poor lifestyle choices. The bottom line seems to be that mental illness is more complicated to understand and people feel less adequately equipped to relate to someone who may be psychotic, hallucinating or experiencing paranoid delusions, which often appear irrational. By writing my memoir and subsequently delivering talks and lectures about my experience of managing patients with severe mental illness, I hoped to shed some more light on this lesser known area of medicine, not in an academic or sensational sense, but at a human and practical level.

This next chapter of my life, following the death of Richard and starting out on my retirement journey, has brought several life lessons. However, it hasn't been without its concern about being judged by others. Did I book my first solo holiday too soon? Do I seem to be enjoying solo travel too much? Am I being insensitive in going away so often when I have a 93-year-old mother back home? As far as Mum goes, that clearly did concern me. I didn't want to be away from her for any protracted period at this time in her life or want her to have less social contact as a result of my travels. It's one thing having carers popping in every day to make her evening meal and personal carers, a cleaner, a hairdresser and a chiropodist popping in on a regular basis, but she needs family contact, social outings and someone to do her shopping.

When I was thinking about signing up to be a cruise line speaker, I spoke to Jill and Fraser to see if they were willing to cover my twice-weekly visits to their gran and do her shopping while I was away. I didn't want my sister to bear the brunt of extra visits. The kids kindly agreed and Mum was delighted to have more contact with her grandchildren. Jill in particular always steps up to the mark as chief shopper, not only for food but also for anything from new summer trousers to a particular brand of hairspray and a trip to the garden centre for afternoon tea. She'll take her friend's dog for a visit, too, and do a wee photoshoot with it, to send to her gran's sister in America.

I was still feeling guilty about the prospect of being away, so I tentatively broached the idea of pursuing a once-a-week placement at a local daycare centre to ensure that Mum had some regular and varied social interaction with people of her own age. To my surprise, she said she'd heard good things about the place I was suggesting, so I made contact. We arranged for a trial day the following week, just before I was due to go on my first lecturing gig organised by the agency in Florida. Spaces don't come up very often, so I suspect some poor soul may have died and we were just lucky with our timing.

You wouldn't believe what my 93-year-old mother has got up to. She's partially sighted due to macular degeneration, and following a stroke and a hip replacement she walks everywhere with a Zimmer frame and has a stairlift in her home. In the past few months, she's had her nails varnished, won an Easter egg at bingo, taken part in quizzes, danced to an Elvis impersonator (with carers holding both her arms for support) and been on a tricycle ride around the Kelpies at Helix Park (she was sitting on a bucket seat with her friend, with someone else pedalling). Having mentioned during a reminiscence chat that she used to be a keen golfer, the staff immediately kicked into action and produced a putting mat, clubs and a ball. Two carers held her steady to free up her arms to hold the club. She could see a line running up the centre of the mat, but her poor vision meant she couldn't see the hole. As she hit the ball, it travelled right up to the edge of the hole but didn't quite go in. One of the carers got down on their knees and tried to blow it in, bless them. She loved it!

My favourite story to date is about the week that the Scotland football team were playing in the European Championships in Germany. She came home literally buzzing with enthusiasm because when they'd arrived at the centre, they'd all been given little plastic hats and a scarf to wear, featuring the Scottish blue-and-white saltire flag. 'We wore the hats for lunch and even when we went to the toilet,' she told me. 'There was a quiz about flags of the countries taking part, but I couldn't really see that. They got out a mat, some goalposts and a ball. We were going to take part in a penalty shootout but I told them I wouldn't be able to kick the ball while standing with my Zimmer frame.' Two carers came to her aid again. They would each get three penalty shootout attempts. Her first attempt was off target. She realised that her poor vision had knocked off her aim, so readjusted her stance and aimed again. She scored and the crowd cheered. Fortunately, she stopped short of pulling her top over her head and running around the pitch like the professional footballers do. That would've been a disaster and probably resulted in another fractured hip!

The following week, she proudly showed off her 'Footballer of the Week' certificate, which she gained for dribbling a football around cones! Despite having fractured her hip several years ago, she still does her physical exercises daily, just to keep herself mobile. The decision to sign Mum up for daycare has given her a new lease of life.

Some of the people at the daycare centre have dementia. In response, Mum asked for some mental agility tests to keep her own mind active. Before bed every night she recites the alphabet backwards and keeps taking seven away from 100 to practise mental arithmetic. How many of you can do that, never mind when you're 93? She's a legend! When I hear her recite these things, it takes me back to the day I took Richard to see the consultant neurologist, just before the scan result that brought our future collapsing down around us. I'd raised concerns about Richard's memory and the consultant formally tested it. Watching him struggle to name as many objects starting with the same letter as he could manage in a minute was so gut-wrenchingly awful. After about five words he just said, 'You've got me there.' He failed to recognise that something was clearly amiss.

On Mother's Day, Mum went to see a Michael Bublé tribute act and had a glass of fizz. Then she went to see Les Misérables at the theatre where Fraser was both director and musical director. I dropped her home at 11.30 pm! Mum embodies the importance of embracing the next chapter of life, whatever age you are. She was widowed suddenly 33 years ago, three months after Jill was born. In later life, she learned to drive, travelled to visit her brother in South Africa and her sister in America, and continued to play competitive bowls and golf until her physical health deteriorated. Despite two strokes, a fractured femur and cardiac bypass surgery (after which she was sent home on her own with a ventilator because her diaphragmatic nerve was damaged and she couldn't breathe properly), she has flourished and embraced life, regardless of her physical frailty and impaired vision. I think I may have inherited some of my drive and determination from her, and for that I'm extremely grateful.

CHAPTER 35

Bookworm

In 2024, I was contacted out of the blue by one of the participants from the Moniack Mhor memoir writing course I attended back in 2018. She wanted to meet up to hear about my author journey as she was feeling a bit stuck with her novel and was looking for some motivation and information about my journey towards publication. We arranged to meet in the coffee shop at Waterstones in Argyle Street, Glasgow, because it seemed like an author-friendly venue. We discussed books, agents, publishers, self-publishing, editors, proofreaders, book coaches, book launches, bookstores, cruising, cruise lecturing, coping with retirement, surviving bereavement, feeling part of a community and everything else in between. It was lovely to catch up again and I was able to put her in touch with fellow author Debra, who does book editing and proofreading, so that felt good too.

When we eventually said our goodbyes, I decided that I'd speak to the store staff to see if they'd consider stocking my book as I'm a local (ish) author. I'd intentionally taken a copy of my book with me, plus an author bio and book summary, kindly prepared by my publisher. The lady told me it would be up to the chief buyer, but she'd take the info to show them. However, when she looked online to confirm that my book was available to order from the store, as I thought it was, she also discovered that physical copies of my book were already stocked in the flagship Sauchiehall Street store in Glasgow. I didn't know that! I headed off to Sauchiehall Street, determined to get a photo of my book on the shelf. It was a huge bookstore over five floors, with lots of subsections. I tried the biography section and then true crime, but failed to locate it, so I approached the librarian, Ian. My book is potentially hard to categorise due to the subject matter, as it could be memoir, biography, medical, psychiatry, mental health or true crime. Ian located it for me at the end of one of the true-crime shelves. Thrilled that he had an author in the store, he asked me to sign a book. He then put a 'signed by the author' sticker on the front, before replacing it on the shelf and asking for a photo he could post on Instagram. I obliged, and asked him to take some for my social media as well. Noting my surprise at finding my book in stock, he beckoned me over to his computer screen. 'It's being stocked in all of our flagship stores across the UK.' Now that was an even bigger surprise! How did I manage to worm my way in there? Perhaps the buyers were influenced by my book sales and where I was sitting in the bestseller list for my genre.

He was impressed that I had an endorsement on the front cover by broadcaster and journalist Leslie Riddoch. That was the first time anyone had commented on my book endorsements, so it was another feather in my author cap. I also shared that I was currently writing book number two. 'We'll do your launch for you next year if you like, free of charge,' he told me. 'We do four to five per week, in the evenings. There's a separate room and a bar. It won't cost you anything and we'll buy books for the event.' Even better. What a productive trip to Glasgow that was.

Meanwhile, I was introduced to the idea of Sip and Swap events by Heather Suttie, a broadcaster, journalist and radio presenter. I can't remember how the initial contact was made, but Heather runs a Facebook group called Book Face, dedicated to sharing positive book reviews and recommendations, and also runs in-person Sip and Swap events where the attendees bring four books to swap. I always take bookmarks as well because you inevitably meet other book lovers, and when they discover I'm an author, it's good to be able to give them something to take away. There's usually a free drink while a well-known author is interviewed by a journalist, followed by a Q&A session and a book signing. I've made it along to several events and they've all been great. I've sometimes taken a copy of my book and given it as a gift to the author interviewee, if the subject matter is relevant to their genre. So far, I've met crime fiction author Val McDermid; Graham Armstrong, who talks about the reality of addiction, youth violence, gang culture and his experiences of growing up in Airdrie; award-winning natural history photographer and documentary filmmaker Doug Allen, who worked with Sir David Attenborough; and finally Guy Greave, Scottish adventurer, entrepreneur and memoirist, who's lived in the wilderness of Alaska.

I gave Val a copy of my book because she writes crime fiction. Maybe I might be of assistance in researching her next book. I also gave Graham a copy, as he's a reformed drug user and gang member who has managed to overcome adversity, achieve academically (he's currently working on his PhD) and become an advisor to the government about service development. He comes from a background similar to many of the clients I dealt with. Much like myself, he believes in people being non-judgemental and the importance of rehabilitation, so I thought he might take something from my book. You never know if these connections will come to anything; only time will tell. I was interested in Doug's and Guy's books because of my travels to Antarctica and Alaska. I bought both of their books and Doug wrote a message in mine about me becoming an Antarctic explorer, which was lovely.

I gave Heather a copy of my book too, and she was kind enough to invite me to be a guest on her podcast, The Book Alchemist. We recorded the podcast at Go Radio studios in Glasgow. In the reception area, I met the interviewee who had been recorded just before me. The lady said she'd heard about my book and was interested in reading it. She introduced herself as Shari Low. I must confess that I didn't recognise her, so I said, 'I've only written one book, have you written many?' Her answer? 'More than 35.' How embarrassing. I found out later that she's a bestselling author of romantic fiction and has a writing partnership with Scottish TV presenter and actor Ross King.

My publisher also introduced me to Sarah Archer, who has a background in stand-up comedy, performance, storytelling, speaking, HR and marketing. She helps people turn their books into impactful keynote speeches. She kindly invited me onto her podcast, The Speaking Club, which is globally successful. I'm so lucky to have made such meaningful connections.

Chapter 36

Home alone

When it came to grief, keeping busy was definitely my coping strategy. I'd tend to only have alone time when I lay in bed at night. On the surface, I looked as if I was coping, but there was one residual issue that took nearly two years to begin improving. As an extrovert, I like being around people and working things through by talking, so I sought out social contact regularly. In the back of my mind, I was concerned about people thinking I didn't care about Richard's death, but the drive to use my normal coping strategy overcame the fear of being judged. I was coping in almost every situation except being alone at home. When Richard was alive, I could settle in the lounge quite happily on my own, as long as I knew he was somewhere in the house. But I recall feeling a bit unsettled if he was on a night out and I was at home alone. I always found it hard to put my finger on it, as I wasn't lonely or scared; I just didn't feel settled. This became acutely exaggerated when he died. There were no outward signs but I was unsettled in the pit of my stomach. And so, I kept busy. I didn't address it until two years later when Fraser temporarily moved out. I couldn't seek alternative social contact as normal as we all had to stay at home because of the Covid restrictions. I stumbled onto pointillism, almost by doodling. Many people use mindfulness colouring books as a way of calming their minds. Some claim it helps them with anxiety, depression and sleep as it can be a way of managing unhelpful thoughts and feelings. What I noticed was that, when I was absorbed in creating pointillism drawings, I was able to sit in my own home and become totally immersed in this focused activity for hours at a time. Gradually, during lockdown, I began to address that residual grief. It would've made more sense for me to acknowledge it and address it long before then and it's sad that it took a pandemic and enforced lockdown to make me do it, but I'm all the better for it. By drawing, I was being active, but the process ensured alone time, to settle me. I find I read a book much more easily now too.

As I process emotions by talking, it helps to chat to my psychotherapist friend Alison. That was a lucky break for me. I found writing my memoir cathartic too, so it comes as no surprise that journaling is one of the things others suggest as a possible coping strategy. I'm fortunate to have stumbled upon pointillism and writing by accident, as I appear to have engaged in mindfulness and a type of journaling. As someone who never reads instructions for anything, it would've been very out of character for me to have looked up any articles for advice on coping with grief or planning retirement. I'm more of a 'trust your gut' kind of gal.

I guess my more introverted friends would've cracked that particular 'being alone in the house' issue before me, but may have struggled more with the enforced social encounters linked to bereavement, such as scores of people popping in to see that you're OK, a large queue of people offering condolences outside the church, dealing with the wake and so on. These were less stressful for me. Ironically, taking time to yourself to process what has happened can be viewed negatively by onlookers. Extroverts may risk being labelled depressed if they take some alone time, as they're not socialising as normal and people notice. Introverts who take more time than usual on their own may even be asked if they're feeling suicidal due to isolation and lack of engagement, but they're having to cope with a double burden and can feel overwhelmed and fatigued by it. The death of a loved one plus the enforced social inter-actions linked to it will deplete their energy resources. This necessitates more alone time, to recharge. My advice is to prioritise self-care. It's a multi-layered, variable and individual process to navigate.

After almost seven years of retirement, I've been trying to train myself to stay in bed until 8.00 am. I still wake at about 5.30 on most mornings, but I think it's important to rest and not be on the go all the time, even though that would probably be my preferred option. I'm making some headway, so you can train an old dog to do new tricks. I also think I may be having my version of the seven-year itch. I started my art business almost seven years ago and it helped greatly with filling my time, providing opportunities for engaging with others, giving me purpose and structure to the week. However, as a result of having chosen to follow the Rotary, writing and enrichment lecturing paths, I now find that I'm really busy, and the art commissions are starting to feel like a bit of a burden. I still enjoy producing art, but working to timescales is much more onerous now because of my busy schedule. I've decided to temporarily close for new commissions and take a break. I've been advocating trying lots of new things and only continuing with the things that make you feel happy and fulfilled, so it's time to practise what I preach.

I've also come to a gradual realisation that if you don't keep the fabric of your home up to date, over time things will gradually start to go wrong or wear out. Come to think of it, that applies to our bodies as well! With this in mind, I've gradually embraced updating certain rooms and furniture. When making decisions about big-ticket items, which I would previously have discussed with Richard, I'm acutely aware that I've lost my sounding board. My view is that it's better to do it now rather than get too old, when the upheaval will feel overwhelming. I have a similar view about long-haul travel. I won't always be fit enough to do it, so I've concluded that I should see as much of the world as I can while I have my health. That's my excuse and I'm sticking to it! I'm not sure my bank balance would agree, though. I still have a bucket list, despite being fortunate to have technically been to all seven continents. A few more countries and destinations will be ticked off in 2025, and I'm always on the lookout for other opportunities.

When I designed the Message of Hope charity cards campaign for Rotary, my desire was for people to write to those who were isolated and bereaved by Covid, to let them know that someone was thinking about them. I decided to write this book as a Message of Hope, Mark II. I hope that sharing the adventures of my journey through bereavement and retirement on to new opportunities will offer hope and inspiration to those who may be struggling at home alone, whatever circumstances have changed in their lives.

CHAPTER 37

Roadmap to retirement

In writing this second memoir, I've had time to reflect on my journey through retirement and why it looks so different from that of some of my friends. I think we all feel fulfilled, which is fortunate, but it's clear that we didn't follow the same roadmap. I guess it's a bit like choosing how to spend your holiday. Some choose to cycle and hike their way around the Highlands of Scotland, sleep in a tent and enjoy meals by a campfire. Some fly business class to five-star luxury resorts in the sun, some go clubbing in Ibiza and others prefer to stay at home, enjoy a bit of gardening and fire up the barbecue for tea. You need different skill sets, levels of fitness, budgets and personality types to get the most out of each. If all constraints regarding health and budgets were magically removed and we were sent to experience a range of holidays, we'd all experience the same holiday very differently. I may be an extrovert, but I don't drink alcohol and do have body image issues. I can think of nothing worse than two weeks on a beach in Ibiza, going to alcohol-fuelled raves in a nightclub until 4.00 am. Downing cocktails and shots as a way of socialising with other partygoers isn't my style.

It's important to identify a roadmap for retirement that suits your circumstances. You may have read about my adventures and thought, 'I can't think of anything worse, travelling solo abroad, meeting thousands of strangers and public speaking in front of hundreds of people.' What if you prefer to sit in the garden, feet up, with a cup of tea and a book, invite your best friend round for a spot of lunch (which you prepared from scratch) and then go to the theatre together in the evening? It's fabulous if you feel fulfilled by this and the built-in time on your own has energised you sufficiently so that you feel recharged and ready to go. I guess the question for anyone entering retirement or any new chapter in life is to ask what type of activities and social connections make you feel energised and fulfilled. You may have to try a few different things and reject some until you find your specific thing, but knowing whether you have more of a tendency towards introversion or extro-version may help to guide your choices.

My friend Alison really enjoys reading, cooking, gardening, learning French and singing, plus putting her feet up with a cuppa. She's perfectly sociable in small and large groups but her preference is to socialise with smaller groups of close friends. Her preferred hobbies are the ones she's developed further during retirement, for example joining a choir and a French class, where she has a shared interest with the group. We're a bit of a yin-and-yang combo. We balance each other out, encourage each other and allow all aspects of our personalities to shine through. She certainly got me reading more and listening to audiobooks in the car, and I've encouraged her to go on more cruises. However, I think we're guilty in equal parts for encouraging each other to visit garden centre restaurants to sample Empire biscuits and rate them out of ten. For the avoidance of any doubt, a crisp biscuit layer with lots of raspberry jam in the middle and a thick, soft icing on top gets top marks from me every time. Just writing this has put me in the mood for another one. I may have to visit the garden centre tomorrow!

When I was working in the community as a forensic psychiatrist, one of the main focuses for our team was to provide a holistic care plan. What does that mean and why am I telling you about it? Holistic care planning means paying attention to all facets of the patient's life as everything potentially impacts a person's mental health and quality of life. Obviously, we had to consider appropriate diagnosis and treatment, but what often meant the difference between engagement and fulfilling lives, or failure to engage, were the other parts of the care plan, for example, housing, financial security, fruitful daytime activity, friendship groups, education, employment, social support, compliance with medication and support with any addiction difficulties.

When I retired and found myself on my own, a holistic care plan was just as important for my wellbeing. I didn't have a multidisciplinary team of professionals around me to manage it, but I needed the same things to be in place, where necessary. I was fortunate that many aspects already were in place, but if they hadn't been, it would've been important to address any issues, to offer me the best chance of an enjoyable, fulfilling retirement. Some of my patients claimed to have lots of pals, but they weren't necessarily a positive influence or support. Some of their acquaintances encouraged substance misuse, antisocial behaviour and financial insecurity. They'd try to exploit more vulnerable patients for money, as they were on higher benefits, by pretending to be their 'friend', which required constant monitoring and intervention. I strongly believe that choosing to be around positive people is crucial. I've given myself permission to seek out friends who are positive, encouraging influences and I actively avoid people who are negative. Positivity attracts and breeds positivity. The new friends I've met throughout my retirement adventures all have that in common. The friendships are not based on age, gender or nationality; we're just enthusiastic people with a zest for life who are attracted to each other's positivity.

What's your snowman?

I f you've ever felt inspired to do some research about how to navigate major life changes and take more control of your life, you'll have found that several common themes emerge. The most important ones for me are mindset and resilience. As I reflect on my own journey, which took me from being 54, married and in full-time employment, to the very next day, when I was 55, widowed and retired, I've identified the factors that have allowed this next chapter of my life to be so positive and rewarding. I've always adopted a glass-half-full mentality, trying to see the positive and potential opportunities in any given situation. This gave me a firm foundation on which to build my future.

What I've learned about myself is that I'm open to change in any given circumstance, seeing it as an opportunity for learning and growth, even if the trigger for the change is unplanned and challenging. It was like this in my workplace, so I applied the same open mind as I adjusted to my new reality as a solo traveller in life. Even positive changes such as a promotion at work can bring adjustments, challenges and difficult emotions. When I became a manager, I experienced a change of colleagues, had to develop new relationships and deal with a change in working dynamics. There was an increase in stress level and responsibility, fear of failure, imposter syndrome, and so on. The time taken to adjust to change is different for everyone, so it's important not to compare. I was initially concerned about how people would judge me for how I dealt with Richard's death, but ultimately I prioritised my mental health and took the steps I needed to get through the process of bereavement. I found that establishing a routine was something I could control and it gave some structure and stability to my week as I made the adjustment from work and my caring role to being on my own and retired.

I've always believed that entering the stretch zone, which lies just outside your comfort zone, is where true learning and development happens, so I approached my new reality in a similar way. I planned to grow as I adjusted to my new reality. If Richard had still been alive, I wouldn't have written and published two books, started an art business or become a cruise line enrichment lecturer. This next chapter of my life wasn't in my retirement plan, but it has turned out to be fabulous. Being open to new opportunities and taking them has been the key. My mantra since Richard's death has been, 'You don't know what's around the corner, so live life to the full today and have no regrets. You're still here.'

I've been supported by friends and family throughout this journey. Managing major life transitions may be difficult, but you don't need to navigate them on your own. Sometimes talking to someone who's dealt with a similar change may be helpful, too. Even in times of adversity, it's important to celebrate the good things in our lives. I hold dear the memories of my 38 years with Richard and the two lovely children we raised. I believe that something good can always come from something bad, and that can help to give closure. That was my aim when carrying out suicide reviews at work as I was always keen to ensure there was positive learning from our reflection to improve services for future patients, even if we couldn't have prevented this particular loss of life.

It's important to focus your attention on the things within your control and not on the past or things outside of your control. These are the things you can influence, as the future hasn't yet been written. Taking some control helps to address negative emotions, feelings of uncertainty and hopelessness. Forward momentum is possible with small, achievable goals. You don't need a grand plan. In fact, I think not having a grand plan is advantageous, as it allows for flexibility and openness to respond to opportunities that may present themselves along the way. I guess we all strive to achieve some emotional fulfilment and having some purpose and meaning will aid this.

Resilience is the ability to bounce back from adversity and maintain a forward momentum. This requires a willingness to tackle situations head on, with a degree of flexibility and emotional maturity. Viewing change as an opportunity rather than a threat can result in truly life-enhancing experiences. I'm fortunate to have developed resilience in my role as a forensic psychiatrist and could draw on this resource in this next chapter of life. For others, it may need some work, but we can all develop skills in this area. Moving from a very emotion-driven, victim mindset to a place where you access your feelings, rational facts and logic at the same time can help you reframe a situation and maintain perspective, as in the old saying, 'When life gives you lemons, make lemonade.'

I also believe that voicing your dreams and ambitions for a positive future makes them more likely to become real. People talk about things like manifesting, coincidence, serendipity and synchronicity. I'm not sure that I totally understand the differences. Manifesting is defined in the dictionary as the act of using methods such as visualisation and affirmation to help you imagine achieving something, in the belief that doing so will make it more likely to happen. It's based on the idea that you can think your dreams into reality. Serendipity, on the other hand, is defined as the occurrence and development of events by chance in a happy or beneficial way. As I understand it, synchronicity seems to be about the alignment of external events with internal experiences, which offers some guidance and insight. It may feel like a personalised message. Unplanned meetings and conversations may introduce you to valuable contacts. To leverage these situations effectively, it's important to remain receptive to new ideas and perspectives arising from unexpected events. In my experience, telling people what I wanted meant that I began to make enabling choices and actively followed up opportunities. This was enhanced by other people helping to make connections for me because they were aware of my aspirations, which ultimately resulted in me achieving my goals. But some of the time I was just in the right place at the right time, by chance. I needed to be open to pursuing the opportunities when they presented themselves, however daunting they felt at the time.

It was like a snowflake that became a snowball with its own momentum, and in no time at all I found myself with a fully fledged snowman. My snowflake was a throwaway comment to a publisher, which, once it had been spoken out loud, resulted in a publishing deal. My snowball was a published memoir and achieving number one on an Amazon bestseller new releases list, which then resulted in an introduction to a cruise line entertainment booker. The snowball was growing and gathering momentum. The snowman that was forming represents me travelling to Antarctica then working as an enrichment lecturer on cruise ships around the world, trying to challenge mindsets and contribute to the destigmatisation of mental illness. I'm having a blast! So, what's your snowflake? If you remain open to the opportunities that life's transitions may afford you, what might your snowman look like?

***

My first memoir, *I Don't Talk to Dead Bodies*, ended on a significant date: 23 March 2018 was my 55th birthday, the day I retired from the NHS and the day my husband Richard died from a brain tumour.

On the same date in 2025, this book was still in production as I spent my 62nd birthday at the hospital with my wonderful 93-year-old mum, saying my final goodbyes. She passed away in the early hours of the next morning.

And so, sadly this book now ends at yet another of life's bookmarks, again on 23 March. It marks the end of another era and a hugely meaningful chapter in my life. Mum was a legend. Her legacy will live on in me, as I create a legacy for my own children. What will your legacy be?

Useful resources

- ★ Andy's Man Club (suicide prevention charity): andysman-club.co.uk
- ★ BACP British Association for Counselling and Psychotherapy: bacp.co.uk
- ★ Business Network International: bni.com
- ★ Counselling Directory: counselling-directory.org.uk
- ★ Cruse Bereavement Support: cruse.org.uk
- ★ MIND mental health charity: mind.org.uk
- ★ Relate relationship counselling: relate.org.uk
- ★ Rotary International: rotary.org
- ★ Royal College of Psychiatrists (information resources): rcpsych.ac.uk
- ★ Samaritans: samaritans.org
- ★ UK Council for Psychotherapy: psychotherapy.org.uk

Further reading

- ★ Morrison, R (2022) *I Don't Talk to Dead Bodies: The curious encounters of a forensic psychiatrist*. Right Book Press.
- ★ Kübler-Ross, E (2014) *On Death and Dying: What the dying have to teach doctors, nurses, clergy & their own families*. Scribner Book Company.

My art

To learn more about my art and writing, visit my website or Facebook pages:

- ★ www.rhonamorrison.com
- ★ Facebook: Rhona Morrison Art, Rhona Morrison Author

Acknowledgements

This memoir, which is part two of my story, has been a joy to write, as the material for it involved living my best life and making memories. It wouldn't have been possible without all the wonderful people who've been part of my retirement journey this far. Friends, family, BNI colleagues, fellow Rotarians, new cruise buddies, cruise line staff, my booking agent Miranda, Ian (who recorded the audiobook version, again) and the team at The Right Book Company. You know who you are.

Special mentions go to the people who've been there at pivotal moments and without whom I wouldn't have made the decision to write that book, become a published author or pursue a career in cruise line enrichment lecturing: Jill, Fraser, my sister Elaine, Louisa, my best friend Alison, Michael Heppell (from Write That Book), Lauren McAlpine (who typed the first draft), Sue Richardson (my publisher), Bev Glick (my wonderful editor), Paul McGinlay (my BNI champion), Duncan Grant (who got me my first speaking gig), Cuddy Cudworth (whose recommendation to a cruise line resulted in me getting my agent Miranda, from Starboard Speakers), and Elaine McCrossan, my Rotary sidekick, who keeps me grounded and engaged in the local community, giving service to others. Without family support and wonderful carers to look after Mum, I wouldn't have been able to pursue my globetrotting adventures in retirement. The rich tapestry of life is made from many threads, each one as integral as each other. Thank you all for being the threads in my unique tapestry.